Mesozoic Era

Cenozoic Era

When the Earth came together as a ball of molten rock, about 4,600 million years ago (mya), it was too hot for anything to live on the surface. It was nearly 1,100 million years before the first life could develop in the Earth's waters.

It took over 2,800 million years for water plants (algae) to pump enough oxygen into the air so that the more complex animals could evolve during the Cambrian Period. However, the first true plants did not appear until the Silurian Period. Between 600 and 225 mya, the invertebrates (which were animals without backbones) evolved. Most live[d in the] sea and a few grew to enormous sizes.

The first vertebrates were fish which [develope]d during the Silurian Period. The amphibians, which lived partly on land, developed during the Devonian Period. The first reptiles, which could live permanentl[y] on land, developed during the Carboniferous Period. Mammals first appeared in the Triassic Period, but it was only in the Tertiary Period that mammals and birds became dominant on Earth. As you can see, human beings did not appear until very recently.

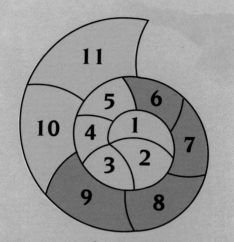

Periods of the World Clock

This symbol is shown alongside every fossil specimen in this book. The dark green segments show you at a glance in which periods of the world the species was alive. In this example the species lived from the Permian to the Cretaceous periods.

1 **Cambrian: 600–500 million years ago**
2 **Ordovician: 500–440 million years ago**
3 **Silurian: 440–395 million years ago**
4 **Devonian: 395–345 million years ago**
5 **Carboniferous: 345–280 million years ago**
6 **Permian: 280–225 million years ago**
7 **Triassic: 225–190 million years ago**
8 **Jurassic: 190–136 million years ago**
9 **Cretaceous: 136–65 million years ago**
10 **Tertiary: 65–2 million years ago**
11 **Quaternary: 2 million years ago to present**

FOSSILS
OF THE WORLD

Chris Pellant

EDITED BY
Andrew Charman

DRAGON'S WORLD

CHILDREN'S BOOKS

Conservation

Fossils are part of the natural world just as much as are butterflies and wild flowers. The plants and animals that live on the Earth today have taken hundreds of thousands of years to adapt to the places in which they live. When we change the landscape, we disturb that adaption. Some creatures can survive such changes. Others cannot, so die out, then the planet has lost them forever.

When you go fossil hunting, try not to damage or disturb the landscape. Remember that the weather breaks up rocks naturally. Fossils may be exposed that were hidden the day before. Above all, help to preserve the landscape so that other people can enjoy it just as you do.

On page 78, you will find the names of some organizations who campaign against unnecessary destruction of the landscape. By joining them and supporting their efforts, you can help to preserve our world and all its creatures.

Fossil Collectors' Code

1 **Always go fossil hunting with a friend.** Always tell an adult where you have gone.
2 **Don't damage the site** and don't take more than one specimen of each fossil – leave something for other collectors.
3 **Wear a hard hat** if you are exploring near a cliff. Check the cliff face carefully before you go near it, because loose rocks sometimes fall on people.
4 **Ask permission before exploring** quarries, sites on private land, or anywhere that you think belongs to somebody else.
5 **Leave fence gates as you find them.**
6 **Take your litter home.** Don't leave it to pollute the countryside.

Dragon's World Ltd
Limpsfield
Surrey RH8 0DY
Great Britain

Published by Dragon's World, 1994

© Dragon's World, 1994
Text © Dragon's World, 1994
Photographs © Chris Pellant, 1994

Illustrations by Mr Gay Galsworthy; headbands by Antonia Phillips.

Simplified text and captions written by Andrew Charman, based on *A Pocket Guide to Fossils* by Chris Pellant.

Editor	Diana Briscoe
Designer	James Lawrence
Art Director	John Strange
Design Assistant	Victoria Furbisher
Editorial Director	Pippa Rubinstein

British Library Cataloguing in Publication Data
The catalogue record for this book is available from the British Library.

ISBN 1 85028 260 9

Typeset in Frutiger Light and Novarese Bold by Dragon's World Ltd.
Printed in Italy.

Contents

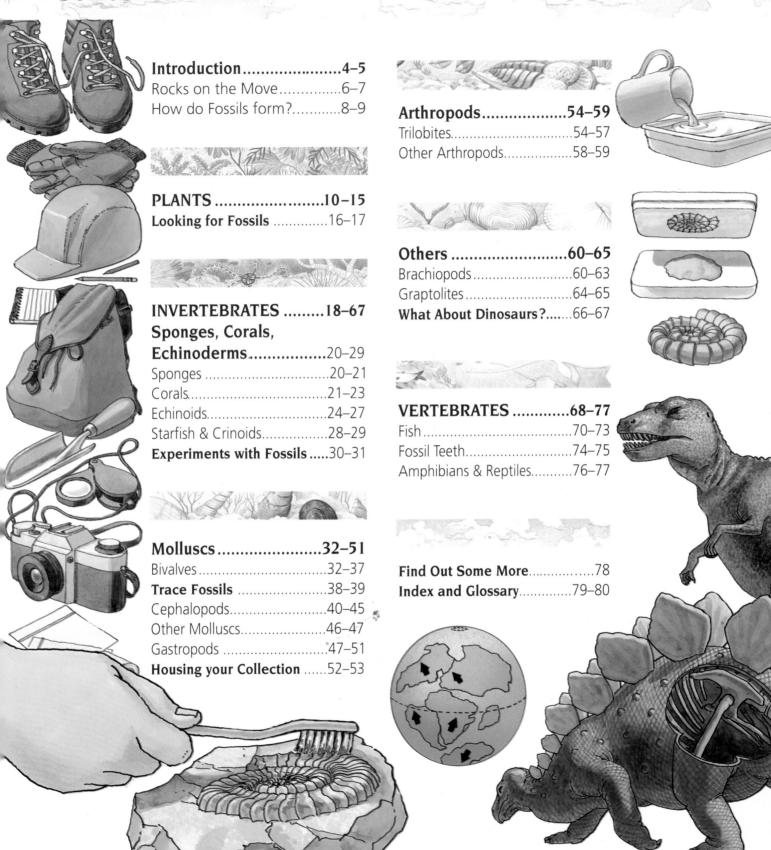

What Are Fossils?

Fossils are what remains of plants and animals that lived millions of years ago. They are a record of past life. A fossil can be the hard parts of a creature, like a shell or a bone. It can also be something that a creature made, like an egg, or a footprint, or a burrow. Sometimes the whole creature is preserved – skin, fur, and all. Insects in amber, or mammoths deep-frozen in ice are examples of these. The usual place to find fossils is in the type of rocks known as sedimentary.

Classification of fossils

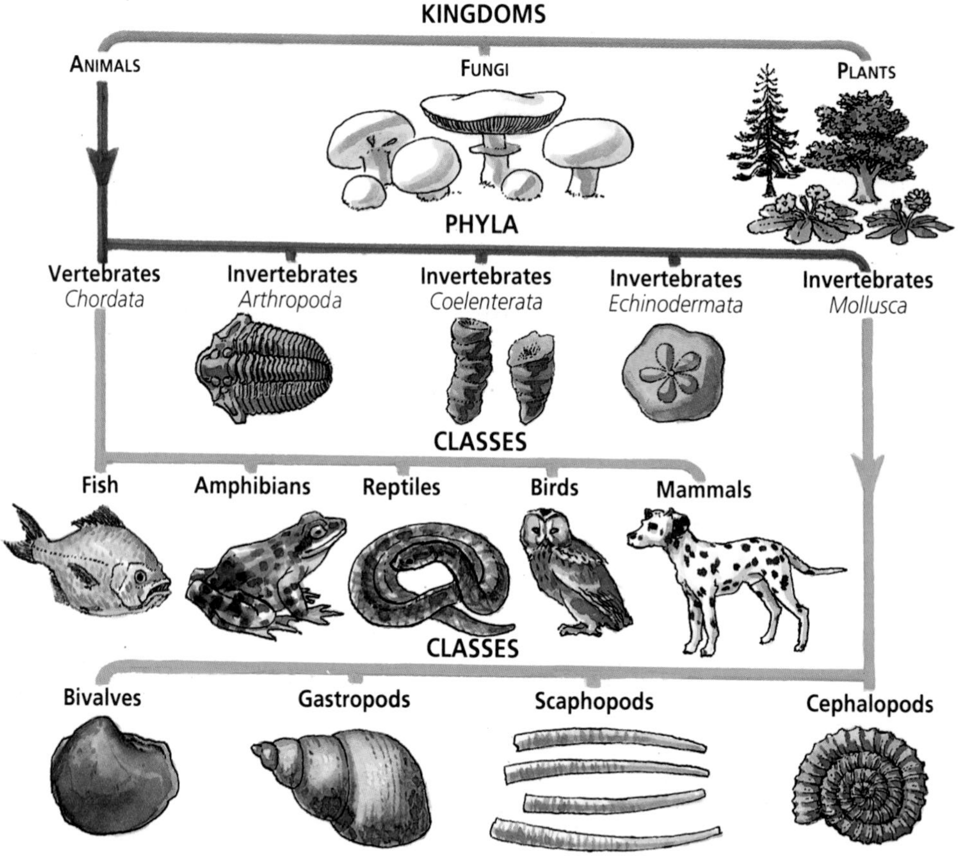

All living things are classified into groups by naturalists. What animal or plant goes into what group is usually based on how it evolved and how it is made. Classification begins by sorting them into the largest, general groups, called **kingdoms**. Then they are sorted into smaller groups, called phyla. The organisms in any group usually share certain features. The last and smallest group in which you can put a creature is its **species**. After that you have individuals.

KINGDOMS

ANIMALS   FUNGI   PLANTS

PHYLA

Vertebrates	Invertebrates	Invertebrates	Invertebrates	Invertebrates
Chordata	*Arthropoda*	*Coelenterata*	*Echinodermata*	*Mollusca*

CLASSES

Fish   Amphibians   Reptiles   Birds   Mammals

CLASSES

Bivalves   Gastropods   Scaphopods   Cephalopods

This picture shows how collectors and scientists classify living things into groups. First they decide which kingdom it belongs to:

Animals   Fungi   Plants

Each kingdom is divided into smaller groups or **phyla** (singular: **phylum**.) Only some of these groups are shown here. In the Animal Kingdom, scientists have to decide if a fossil falls into:

Vertebrates   or   Invertebrates

If the fossil is a vertebrate, it might be from any of the five main **classes** – fish, amphibians, reptiles, birds, or mammals. So they must compare it to other fossils that they know about, and living creatures, to decide where it should be put. As they work through the various levels of classification, more and more animals are eliminated until they either identify its species, or decide that the fossil needs to be classified as a new species.

4

Breaking up & settling down

Weather breaks up rocks into small grains, called **sediments**. Then rivers carry these sediments to the sea. There the sediments sink to the bottom and are scattered over the sea bed. New sediments are scattered on top. The earlier and lower layers, or **strata**, are squashed and cemented together to form rock.

Layers of sedimentary rock are being laid down all the time. They are forming now in rivers and sea beds. Bodies of dead creatures are falling on to these beds and being buried by new layers – they are the fossils of the future.

The wind, sun, and rain wear away the rocks. ——

Sediments are carried down to the sea by rivers and streams. ——

The sediments settle on the sea bed in layers.

Pressure from the water above cements the sediments into hard rock. ——

How this book works

The opening pages of this book show how sedimentary rocks are formed and how fossils are made. The book then describes the many different kinds of fossils. They are grouped together using the same methods that scientists use to classify living creatures. The first section is on **plants**. The second section is on **invertebrates** (creatures that do not have a bony skeleton inside their bodies). The last section is on animals that do have an internal skeleton of bones – called **vertebrates**.

Top-of-Page Picture Bands

Each group of creatures has a different picture band at the top of the page. These are shown below. They will help show you which section of the book you are in.

Plants

Sponges, Corals, & Echinoderms

Molluscs

Arthropods

Brachiopods

Vertebrates

Rocks on the Move

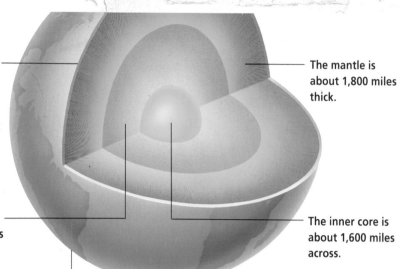

The surface of the Earth is never still. Nothing stays the same for very long. Weather patterns change, rivers and glaciers follow different courses, mountains thrust up, seas rise and fall. Some of these changes take place because the Earth's rocks are moving.

Some sedimentary rocks are pushed down by Earth movements to areas where temperatures are very high. There they melt and may come to the surface again as molten rock (or **lava**). Others are pushed up to form hills or mountains. They are twisted, or folded, or even turned upside-down. Then they may be exposed to the sun, wind, and rain. They start to break up and the cycle has begun again.

The Earth's crust is 25 miles thick, or can be more, underneath the continents. But it is only about 5 miles thick underneath the oceans.

The outer core is about 1,400 miles thick.

The mantle is about 1,800 miles thick.

The inner core is about 1,600 miles across.

Under our feet

The Earth is actually made of layers. The top layer on which we live is the Earth's **crust**. Below this is a thick layer called the **mantle**. Deeper still is the **outer core** which is probably made of molten iron and nickel. In the centre of the Earth is the **inner core** which scientists think is a solid ball of iron and nickel. The further down into the earth you go, the hotter it gets. The temperature in the centre is about 9,000° Fahrenheit.

Floating plates

The crust and the upper part of the mantle are divided into sections called plates. These plates float on the hot, plastic rocks underneath them. About 200 million years ago the Earth's land mass was one large continent. This broke up about 150 million years ago and the continents that we know today started to drift away from each other. They moved into the general pattern of today's world about 65 million years ago. They are still moving by a few inches every year.

200 million years ago there was just one large continent called Pangaea.

150 million years ago the one continent split into smaller ones.

65 million years ago the continents formed the arrangement we know today.

Uplifting rocks

When these floating plates run into each other, they sometimes push up rocks to make mountains. Other rocks are forced down under the oceans. Earthquakes happen when plates rub against each other. Volcanoes are weaknesses in the joins between plates where molten rock (**magma**) from below escapes to the surface as lava.

The movements of the land cause sea levels to change. Deserts can become sea beds and ocean floors can become mountain ranges. This is why fossils of sea-living creatures can be found on mountain tops.

One day, these drifting continents will meet once again to form one large land mass. This repeating pattern is believed to have happened several times in the 4,600 million years that the Earth has existed. Each pattern or cycle is thought to take about 440 million years.

100 million years from today the continents will have moved into a new pattern. The arrows show the direction in which the continents are moving today.

Folding and faulting

Sedimentary rocks build up layer upon layer. The oldest layers are those lower down, and the youngest are at the top. Unfortunately, they do not stay in this neat arrangement. As the land masses move, so the layers buckle and fold. This makes it difficult to match layers in two different areas, but it does push fossil-bearing rocks to the surface. Faults happen when the rock has broken and the two sides of the break slip away from each other.

Exposed by erosion

Wind, water, and ice wear away rocks as they move. This is called **erosion**. Sedimentary rocks are quite soft and are worn away easily. Water is a powerful force—rough seas can eat away at cliff faces, rivers can carve deep valleys. When this happens the layers of sedimentary rock are exposed, and so are the fossils within them.

Fossil-bearing rocks are also exposed by the activities of people. When we dig quarries or cut through rocks to lay new roads or railroads, the layers in sedimentary rock are exposed. The unwanted rubble left by the bulldozers may contain fossils. You should always get permission before collecting fossils in places like these.

How Do Fossils Form?

Thousands of millions of living things have existed on Earth, but only a small number of them ever became fossils. Most sediments are laid down at sea, so most fossils are of creatures which lived and died in the sea.

A creature is more likely to be preserved as a fossil if it has some hard parts. These might be bones or a shell. These hard parts will survive being knocked or jolted in the time it takes for a layer of sediment to cover them.

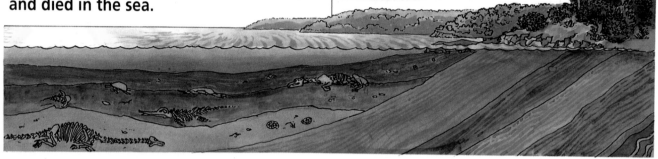

Turning to stone

There are several different ways in which fossils are formed. Many are turned to stone: the substance of which the shell or bone was made is replaced by new minerals, like pyrite or quartz. This is called **petrification**. Minerals are the natural components that make up the rocks of the Earth.

These minerals are washed into the fossil as they are carried through the surrounding rock by liquids seeping through it. The liquids running through the rock can also dissolve or wash away the shell. This then leaves a hollow where the hard part once was. The hollow, or mould, is then filled in by different minerals. This is known as a **fossil cast**.

Organic sedimentary rock is made up mainly of fossils with just a little rock to hold them together. Shelly limestone is a term used to describe limestone that is rich in fossils. One small sample of this rock may contain many different fossils.

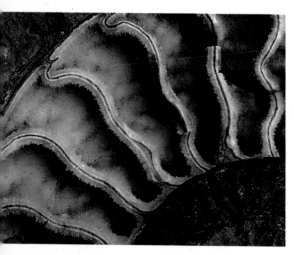

Tree cross-section, filled with opal

Fossil cast

Shelly limestone

Fossils help to date rocks

Sedimentary rocks can buckle and fold due to pressures from beneath the crust, but it is still possible to work out in which order they were laid down. Fossils can help us to do this.

Some ancient creatures existed for only a short time, so their fossils appear only in certain layers. We can use the fossils to work out how old these layers are. Then, if we find a fossil of that creature again, in another place, we can be certain of the age of the rocks in which we found it. Fossils that help us to do this are known as **zone** fossils.

Free-swimming, sea-living creatures make very good zone fossils. They spread out through the oceans to many different parts of the world. They help us to date and relate rocks which may be many hundreds or thousands of miles apart.

This ammonite (*Psiloceras planorbis*) is one of the zone fossils for the Jurassic period.

Insects in amber

Not all fossils are turned to stone. Some are found exactly as they were in life. Insects and plant seeds are sometimes preserved in amber, which was originally the sticky resin of a pine tree. Insects were trapped in the resin flow and buried undamaged. Later the tree died and rotted away, and the insect and the resin became fossilized.

Clues to the past

Evolution is an explanation of the process by which plants and animals have changed over time to what they are now. These changes make the creatures more able to survive. Evolution usually occurs over long time periods, but some creatures and plants have gone through rapid changes that produced new species. Fossils show us what changes groups of creatures have gone through.

Fossils can also tell us about ancient environments. This is done by comparing fossil creatures to their relatives living today. For example, present-day corals live in warm, shallow seas. So it is likely that fossil corals (see pages 21–23) lived in the same kind of environment.

Plants

When the Earth came together as a ball of molten rock, about 4,600 million years ago (mya), it was too hot for anything to live on the surface. It took over 1,100 million years before the first life that has been well fossilized – blue-green algae – could develop in the Earth's waters.

These algae are still to be found today; their fossils are called Stromatolites. All green plants give off oxygen (the gas that all living creatures breathe) as they make their food. It took over 2,800 million years for the algae to pump enough oxygen into the air so that the very first animals could evolve. It took about another 250 million years before the first true plants, like *Cooksonia*, appeared during the Silurian Period.

By about 370 mya, during the Devonian Period, the new continents were covered in plants and forest. The plants were very small by our standards – the ceiling of the forest was only about 1m above the ground. However, they gave off a lot of oxygen and the improved air allowed more complex plants and animals to develop.

During the Carboniferous Period (345–280 mya), the swampy, lowland areas of the continents were covered with very large ferns, and the first trees appeared. Conifers and ginkgos became common about 150 mya and the first flowers appeared at the end of the Jurassic Period, about 140 mya.

Many modern types of plants developed during the Cretaceous Period (136–65 mya). Because these plants were so like their modern relatives, scientists can discover how the climate (rainfall and long-term temperature) have changed in the last 65 million years. Everything we know today about how life on Earth has developed has come from studying fossils.

Plants

Alethopteris

These plants are seed ferns. Fossils of them are found as thin films of black carbon between layers of shale. The carbon is all that is left of the original plant. The leaves have a central stem with small leaflets along both sides.

Size: This specimen is 82mm long
Distribution: North America & Europe
Time range: Carboniferous

Calamites

These fossils are parts of plants called horsetails. They are a section of the stem. The centre of the stem was once filled with soft tissue called pith. This rotted away quickly when the plant died. The hollow stem then filled with sand. The fossil is a cast of that hollow stem. The markings running along its length are imprints of the vessels which used to carry water along the stem. Fully grown plants were up to 20 m high and shaped like Christmas trees.

Size: Section shown is about 120mm long
Distribution: North America, Europe, & Asia
Time range: Carboniferous and Permian

Cooksonia

These are important fossils. *Cooksonia* was one of the first plants to have vessels in its stem for carrying water and other fluids. At the end of the stems were spore-cases. These released spores into the air. New plants could grow from the spores, but only if the spores landed on moist ground. This is why this tiny plant lived in swampy places. It had no leaves, but there were roots which helped to secure it in the swampy ground.

Size: This specimen is 70mm across
Distribution: North America, Europe, Africa, Asia, & Antarctica
Time range: Silurian to Devonian

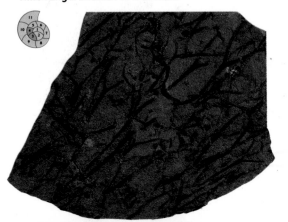

Sphenopteris

Only the leaves of this plant are commonly found as fossils. It can be a fern or a seed fern. It is thought that it was a plant living in marshy places. The leaflets have slightly toothed edges.

Size: This specimen is 63mm long
Distribution: Worldwide
Time range: Carboniferous to Permian

Lepidodendron

These fossils are actually part of a giant clubmoss. Over 100 different kinds of clubmoss have been found, and they once formed dense forests. The remains of these forests are preserved as coal. The fossil of a stem, shown here, has diamond-shaped markings on it. This is where the leaves were once joined to the stem.

Size: Up to 30.5m tall, with a stem 990mm across
Distribution: Europe, north Africa, & Asia
Time range: Upper Carboniferous

Eupecopteris

These seed ferns are commonly found fossils. The plants had woody stems and delicate leaves. Each leaf has a straight, central stem with egg-shaped leaflets along both sides. This specimen shows one leaf. It was found inside a 'nodule' (or lump) of ironstone. The nodule was formed within sedimentary rock.

Size: This specimen is 63mm long
Distribution: Europe, North America, & Asia
Time range: Upper Carboniferous

Mariopteris

A fern which produced spores. When spores land on moist ground, they grow into a green bloom of tissues called a 'prothallus'. This eventually grows into a new fern plant. The large leaves of *Mariopteris* are arranged in a spiral down the central stem. The leaflets of each leaf are narrow and have toothed edges.

Size: This specimen is 57mm long
Distribution: North America & Europe
Time range: Carboniferous

Plants

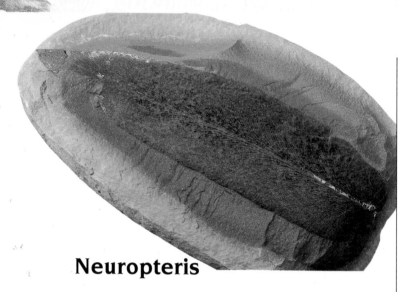

Neuropteris

This seed fern is usually preserved as a thin film of carbon between layers of sediment (see page 8). Often the leaflets are no longer attached to the central stem of the leaf. This plant lived in swamps where gradually many layers of peat built up. This later became compressed and turned into coal.

Size: Leaves are about 50mm long
Distribution: North America & Europe
Time range: Upper Carboniferous

Acer

This group of trees can still be found today. It includes the maples and the sycamores. These trees have flowers. Flowering plants did not develop until the end of the Jurassic period, but then developed very quickly and soon became the dominant kind of plants on Earth. This fossil is of a leaf from an *Acer*. Such fossils are formed only where soft, fine sediments are laid down quickly.

Size: This specimen is 57mm wide
Distribution: Worldwide
Time range: Late Tertiary

Coniopteris

A thin layer of black carbon is often all that remains of the soft plant tissues of ferns (see page 8). There is a central stem with leaflets growing out at an angle. The leaflets are toothed on the upper edges.

Size: Leaves are 20mm long
Distribution: northernmost North America, CIS, India, Japan, & Europe
Time range: Triassic to Cretaceous

Williamsonia

This plant belongs to a group known as the cycads. They are shrubs and trees that look like thick-stemmed palms, and still survive today in tropical regions. They once formed forests with ginkgos and conifers. This fossil shows the leaflets along either side of the leaf's central stem. It has been preserved as a thin, black layer of carbon.

Size: This specimen is 3.2cm long
Distribution: Worldwide – Time range: Jurassic

Ginkgo

This tree can still be seen today in many parks and gardens. It grows wild only in China. Fossils show that it has not changed for 150 million years; for this reason it is known as a living fossil. There are male and female *gingko* trees. Male pollen is formed on catkins. It is then blown by the wind to the female trees. Only after this can the female trees develop seeds.

Size: Leaf is 3.2cm across
Distribution: Once
Europe, Asia, and
North America;
now only China
Time range: Permian
to Quaternary

Algae

These plants were among the first living things to exist on Earth. At that time there was no oxygen in the Earth's atmosphere. It would not have been a suitable place for air-breathing animals to live. Like all plants, algae produce oxygen. They changed the Earth's atmosphere and helped to make it a planet fit for more complex life. Many algae live in the sea. Some are more commonly known as seaweeds.

Solenopora

This is another group of algae. Like the stromatolites, it may form a mound, or may be a slender, tube-like structure. The tubes have Y-shaped branches, covered with many fine holes, or pores. They are made of calcite.

Size: Area shown is 38mm across
Distribution: Worldwide
Time range: Ordovician to Jurassic

Stromatolite

This is the fossil of a lime-rich material which is secreted by blue-green algae. The material forms curved, layered mounds. These are easily fossilized because they are almost rock to begin with. Strings of these mounds, many miles in length, form in shallow seas. The oldest of these fossils are 3,500 million years old, but such mounds are still being formed today. Stromatolites vary in size; they can be up to 500mm high.

Size: This specimen is 20mm across; the double
mound is 101mm across – Distribution: Worldwide
Time range: Pre-Cambrian to Quaternary

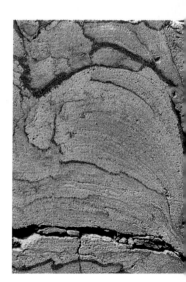

Looking for Fossils

You may want to look for fossils in your local area or somewhere farther away. You can start by writing to the nearest geological survey agency. It should have listings or guides to significant fossil sites in the area and what they contain. You can also find out about an area by reading guide books, asking your local reference librarian to track down helpful publications, and visiting local museums.

If possible, always go on a field trip with someone who knows about fossils, like a teacher or an experienced collector. They can tell you what you have found. Also, join your local geological or fossil society (see page 78); this is the best way to learn in the field.

Geological maps

A geological map will show you what rocks are at the surface and where they are (geology is the study of rocks, minerals, and fossils). The different rocks are shown as different colours. Contour lines show the height of the ground above sea level. You can use them to look for steep hillsides where the rocks have been eroded. These are good fossil-hunting places. Rivers, roads, railways and quarries are also shown.

It is a good idea to get to know what the different kinds of rocks look like. Sedimentary rock is the most important to the fossil hunter (see page 5). Limestones from the bottom of the sea, and shale from the mud laid down in the sea are the best rocks to look for.

Folds and faults

Sedimentary rocks are folded and twisted as the Earth's crust moves. This pushes to the surface rocks which may otherwise have stayed deep inside the Earth. These rocks need to be broken up and exposed before we can find the fossils within them.

This happens in several different ways. A fault occurs when an area of rock splits and the two sides slip away from each other. This may expose a cliff face of rock strata. Rocks are continually being exposed and worn away by the weather. Water is the main element at work here. Rivers and streams carve valleys through the landscape; seas eat away at the land's edge. This results in steep-sided gullies and sea-cliffs where the rock strata are exposed. As the rock is worn away, fossils simply drop out of it and fall to the ground.

People also expose rocks. Whenever we dig quarries or build new roads and railroads, we open up parts of the Earth's surface. These places are good for finding fossils, but never go on to sites like this without getting permission in advance.

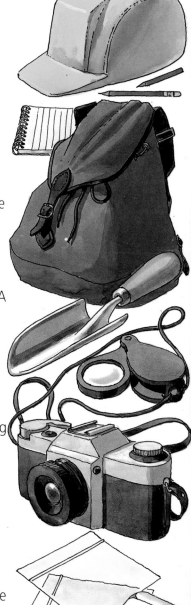

Extracting fossils

The best places to look for fossils are where weathering is taking place. Fresh fossils are falling from the layers all the time. There is no need to damage the rocks to reach them.

1 **Break off unwanted rock** if possible, so that the specimen is easier to carry home.

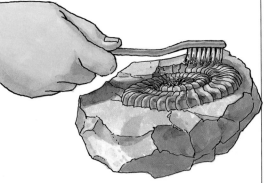

2 **Some fossils only need to be brushed clean.** Others need to be brushed or scraped to remove unwanted sediments. Be careful that your tools do not damage the fossil. Work gently so as not to break the specimen.

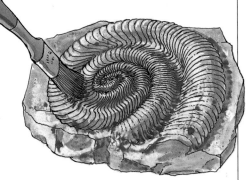

3 **Paint the specimen with varnish** to protect it.

What you need

1 **Footwear:** walking boots are best, but strong trainers laced up properly will protect your feet and ankles against loose or sharp rocks.

2 **Clothes:** in hot weather make sure you have light clothes to protect you from sunburn. If it is likely to rain or be cold, wear waterproof or warm clothes. Listen to the weather forecasts.

3 **Gloves:** you need a strong pair to protect your hands from sharp rock fragments.

4 **Hard hat or other protective headgear:** wear a hard hat if you are near cliffs or places where there may be falling rock. You may feel silly, but you will be safer.

5 **Lightweight backpack:** this is the most comfortable way to carry your equipment and finds, and leaves your hands free.

6 **Field notebook with pencils and pens:** make notes of the date, the weather, where you go, what you find, and the rocks that it came from so that you can write up your fossil diary later.

7 **Hand lens:** buy one that is ten power (labelled x10), and wear it on a cord around your neck. A rock store or museum shop will have one.

8 **Trowel:** for digging specimens out of earth falls. But don't use it to pry fossils out of the rock because you may damage them. You can find loose specimens very easily on most sites.

9 **Camera:** if you take photographs of fossils, rather than prying them out, it avoids damaging the environment.

10 **Bags and containers:** take strong cloth bags for large specimens. Small, self-sealing, plastic bags are good for small specimens. Newspaper and bubble wrap are useful for protecting delicate fossils.

11 **Small notepad or a roll of 4 x 8 cm self-adhesive labels:** they are easier to use for notes about your specimens than trying to write on the bag itself.

Invertebrates

Invertebrate is a general name to describe a huge range of animals that do not have internal backbones. Some of them, like worms or jellyfish, have no backbone at all. Others, like seashells, insects and lobsters, have exoskeletons (outside hard cases or shells).

The first invertebrate fossils date from about 700 million years ago (mya). These worm- and jellyfish-like animals descended from more primitive (basic) animals. Their bodies only very rarely formed fossils.

It was not until invertebrates started making shells for themselves at the start of the Cambrian Period (600–500 mya) that many fossils appear. Probably animals did not make themselves shells before that because there were not enough of the right minerals in the seawater.

Between 600 and 225 mya (the end of the Permian Period), all the groups of invertebrates featured in this book evolved. Most of them lived in the sea and many grew to enormous sizes. As plants colonized the land in the Devonian period (395–345 mya), invertebrates evolved which could live on dry land. Huge dragonflies hunted in the swamps of the Carboniferous Period. By the time the first vertebrates ventured on to dry land, there were plenty of invertebrates for them to eat.

Invertebrates continued to evolve during the Jurassic and Cretaceous Periods. Winged insects increased shortly after the first flowering plants appeared. In the seas, the molluscs evolved in many different ways. A most successful group was the ammonites with over 12,000 species – the largest grew to over 3.6m across. They became extinct about 65 mya in the unknown catastrophe that ended the Cretaceous Period.

Sponges & Corals

Sponges live today in both salt and fresh water. They have a bag-like structure with an opening on the upper surface. There is often a long stalk underneath.

Water goes into the sponge through a hole in the centre of the 'bag'. The creature takes food from it and oxygen for breathing. The skeleton of a sponge is made up of hard spiky structures called 'spicules'. These are well preserved as fossils.

Thamnospongia

These fossils are shaped like a crooked root. Their outer surface is rough and covered with tiny holes, or pores. This specimen was found inside a lump of flint – a stone, made of silica, that is hard and breaks with dangerously sharp edges. It is thought that this silica is formed from the skeletons of sponges which died millions of years ago.

Size: This specimen is 82mm across
Distribution: Worldwide – Time range: Cretaceous

Siphonia

These tulip-shaped sponges were fixed to the sea bed by 'roots', which are not usually preserved. The rounded part has many small pores which lead to canals inside. These join a large canal which reaches from the upper surface to the centre. The smaller canals bring water into the sponge, the larger one removes it. The sponge takes food and oxygen from this water.

Size:
This specimen is
30mm long
Distribution: Europe
Time range:
Cretaceous to
Tertiary

Ventriculites

Sponges belonging to this genus are shaped like narrow vases. Some of these fossils can be found complete with roots. The walls of the sponge are thin. There are grooves running up and down and from side to side over the surface. The skeleton of spicules has six branches. Present-day relatives of this genus live in warm European seas.

Size:
This specimen is
30mm long
Distribution: Europe
Time range:
Cretaceous

Corals are made up of tube-shaped structures called 'corallites'. At the top of each corallite is a shallow, bowl-shaped hollow. This is where a soft-bodied creature, called a 'polyp', lives. The polyp makes the corallite by producing a material called calcite.

The corallite is divided into chambers inside by plates, called 'tabulae'. There are also walls which go from top to bottom, called the 'septa'. They grow outward from the centre to the outside walls. From above, they form a pattern like the spokes of a bicycle wheel. Some corals live alone; others live in large groups called colonies.

Favosites

This coral is made up of many small, closely packed corallites living in a colony, which can be up to 406mm across. The outline of the colony is rounded. From above you can see that the corallites have several straight sides. This is called 'polygonal cross-section'. It makes the colony look like a piece of honeycomb. *Favosites* is now extinct. It lived in shallow seas.

Size: This specimen is 89mm across
Distribution: Worldwide
Time range: Upper
Ordovician to
Middle
Devonian

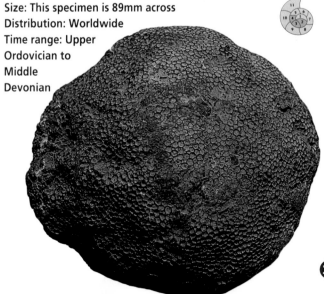

Thamnopora

This is an extinct coral. It grew outward in many branches to about 355mm across. The photograph shows a specimen which has been cut through and polished. The tabulae show up as thin, pale lines within each corallite.

Size: Area shown is 82mm across
Distribution: Worldwide – Time range: Devonian

Dibunophyllum

These corals lived alone and not in a colony; they could grow up to 30mm across. The genus is now extinct. This specimen has been cut through so that the septa can been seen as lines going into the centre from the outer edge. Some go right into the centre, others do not. The outside walls are thickened by web-like masses of calcite called 'dissepiments'.

Size: This specimen is 19mm across
Distribution: North America, Asia, Europe, & north Africa
Time range: Lower Carboniferous

Corals

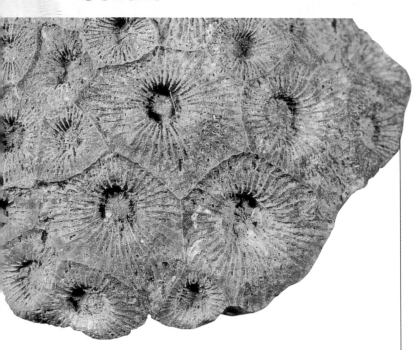

Thysanophyllum

This coral lived in colonies. Each corallite is joined closely to its neighbours. They have angular outlines of six or eight sides. The septa reach almost to the middle of the corallites. The outside walls are thickened by dissepiments (membranes).

Size: This specimen is 101mm across
Distribution: Europe – Time range: Carboniferous

Lithostrotion

This coral formed a colony which looks like a mass of roots. There are tabulae and septa. The central parts are cone-shaped. These fossils are common in limestone rocks and calcite-containing shales (a type of rock that splits easily into fine layers).

Size: This specimen is 70mm across
Distribution: Europe, North America, north Africa, & Australia
Time range: Carboniferous

Cyathophyllum

These corals lived alone and are now extinct. They vary in shape from long and thin to cone-shaped. The septa stretch from the centre to the outside walls. They can be seen as thin lines on the long, thin specimen in the photograph. The hollow on the top of the coral is very shallow.

Size: The long, thin specimen is 70mm long
Distribution: North America, Europe, Asia, & Australia
Time range: Devonian

Ketophyllum

The photograph shows two halves of one specimen. The half on the left shows how it is made inside. This coral is cone-shaped. The hollow in the top is deep, and there are ridges on the outside. The septa do not reach the middle. The tabulae can be clearly seen. It was fixed to the sea bed with root-like structures, which are sometimes preserved.

Size: This specimen is 82mm long
Distribution: Europe & China
Time range: Silurian

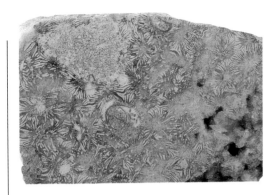

Londsdaleia

This extinct coral lived in colonies. There is a deep dip on the top of each corallite where the polyp lived. There is also a central column running from top to bottom. The septa reach right up to the central column.

Size: Each corallite is about 8mm across
Distribution: North America, Europe, Asia
north Africa & Australia
Time range: Carboniferous

Thamnastrea

This specimen has been cut through. The corallite walls are not well formed; they seem to join with each other. This coral often formed large masses which branched outward. It built reefs with other corals such as *Isastraea* – these reef coral masses could reach 1m 37cm across. It is often preserved in oolitic limestone.

Size: The area shown is 51mm across
Distribution: North & South America, Europe, & Asia
Time range: Triassic to Cretaceous

Thecosmilia

This coral lived in warm, shallow seas and was a reef builder. The septa are straight walls of calcite spreading out like rays from the centre. They are in groups of six. The outside walls of each corallite are made stronger by dissepiments. It is often fossilized in oolitic limestones. In the top photograph the small round ooliths (grains of rock) can be seen.

Size: The single, whole specimen is 32mm wide
Distribution: Worldwide
Time range: Triassic to Cretaceous

Isastraea

In this coral, the six-sided corallites lived closely joined in large colonies. The septa (see page 21) grew in groups of six. Some of them are long and reach all the way from the edge to the centre. The colony itself is a rough tube-shape, narrower at the bottom than at the top. This is a reef-building coral.

Size: The whole coral is 64mm tall
Distribution: Europe, North America, & Africa; this specimen is from southern England
Time range: Jurassic to Cretaceous

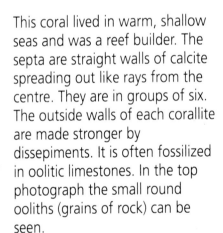

Sea Urchins

The soft body of a sea urchin is safely protected inside its shell, or 'test'. This test can vary considerably in shape. It may, in some species, be rounded, and in others it is heart-shaped.

The test is made of bands of plates of two types, which usually run from top to bottom around the animal. The narrower bands ('ambulacra') are made of plates having pores (small holes) in them. Broader bands, running between the ambulacra, are called the 'interambulacra'. In living species, there are delicate tube-feet, used for moving, feeding and breathing, that pass through the pores.

'Regular' sea urchins have a shell that appears to be divided into five segments. The mouth is centred underneath the body and the anus (waste-expelling hole) is on top. 'Irregular' sea urchins may have their mouth and anus on the side of the shell, and their ambulacra vary in shape. Many sea urchins have masses of spines covering the shell, but these often break off before the fossil forms. Sea urchins are common sea creatures today.

Holectypus

This sea urchin has a round test which looks slightly domed when seen from one side. The underside, where the mouth is, is flat or slightly hollowed, and has several large swellings. This is an irregular urchin, because the anus is on the same side as the mouth and off-centre. The ambulacra are fairly straight, and reach all the way round from the upper to the lower surface.

Size: This specimen is 19mm across
Distribution: Europe, North America, north Africa, & Japan
Time range: Lower Jurassic to Upper Cretaceous

Cidaris

This specimen has been preserved with its spines, which makes it an unusual fossil. Usually the test and the spines are preserved separately. This is a regular sea urchin. The mouth and anus are in the centre of the lower and upper surfaces respectively.

Size: This specimen is 32mm across
Distribution: Worldwide – Time range: Jurassic to Quaternary

Cassidulus

This is a small, irregular sea urchin. The outline of the test is almost round, but looks as though it has five sides. The ambulacra are petal-shaped and do not reach all the way around the test. They form a star shape on the upper surface. The anus can be seen at the edge of the left side of the specimen.

Size: This specimen is 38mm across
Distribution: Worldwide
Time range: Tertiary to Quaternary

Holaster

This sea urchin is irregular. The test is heart-shaped with a slightly domed upper surface, and a slight point at the rear end. The ambulacra are petal-shaped and have slit-shaped pores arranged in pairs. The interambulacra are broad. There are small swellings on the upper surface, larger ones below.

Size: This specimen is 89mm across
Distribution: Worldwide
Time range: Lower Cretaceous to Tertiary

Size: Up to 38mm across
Distribution: North America, especially California
Time range: Tertiary to Quaternary

Dendraster

This is a common genus of irregular sea urchins. Often they form a large part of the rock in which they are found. The fossils are oval in outline and very flat. They are known as 'sand dollars'. The ambulacra are petal-shaped and do not reach all the way around the test. They start at a point which is at the rear end of the upper surface. The anus is on the outside edge of the under surface. There is a groove above it.

Echinocorys

This is an irregular sea urchin with a domed upper surface and a flat base. The anus is on the lower surface. The ambulacra are quite straight and have their pores arranged in pairs. A ridge runs across the test between the mouth and anus. The wide interambulacra have small swellings. *Echinocorys* may have lived partially buried in the sea bed.

Size: This specimen is 83mm across
Distribution: North America, Europe, & Asia
Time range: Upper Cretaceous

Sea Urchins

Clypeaster

This genus contains the largest known sea urchins. They are still to be found today in shallow, warm seas where they burrow into the sea bed. The irregular test is roundish, almost five-sided. The short ambulacra are raised slightly and form a flower pattern. The mouth and anus are both on the flattened underside. There are five furrows leading to the mouth, which has strong jaws. They eat pieces of plant and animal material which they sift from the sea-bed sediment.

Size: This specimen is 70mm across
Distribution: Worldwide
Time range: Upper Tertiary to Quaternary

Hemipneustes

A large and irregular sea urchin. The smooth test is round or oval and looks domed from the side. The anus is at the rear end, the mouth toward the front. There is a groove on the test. One of the ambulacra is in this groove.

Size: This specimen is 63mm across
Distribution: Northern Europe
Time range: Cretaceous

Clypeus

A large and irregular sea urchin. The anus is to be found on the upper surface of the test in a groove, while the overall shape of the test is flattened. The ambulacra are slightly petal-shaped and reach all the way around the test. The pores are slit-shaped, and the interambulacra have smaller pores as well.

Size: This specimen is 70mm across
Distribution: Europe, Africa, & Australia – Time range: Jurassic

Amphiope

This strange, flattened, irregular sea urchin has a round outline. There are two notches at the rear end. The under surface (shown on the right) is covered in small pores. There are Y-shaped grooves going outward from the mouth. The anus is between the notches on this surface. On the upper surface the ambulacra make a flower shape.

Size: Up to 32mm across
Distribution: Europe & India – Time range: Tertiary

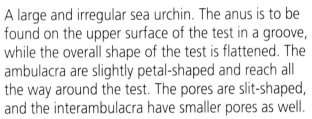

Parmulechinus

This irregular sea urchin was small, round, and very flat. The short, petal-shaped ambulacra form a flower-like pattern on the upper surface. There are pores along their edges. The mouth is to be found in the centre of the underside.

Size: This specimen is 12mm across
Distribution: Europe & north Africa
Time range: Tertiary

Encope

These irregular sea urchins lived in huge numbers on the sea bed. They live today in waters as shallow as 228m. There are holes at the end of the petal-shaped ambulacra. Another hole can be seen on the upper surface. The mouth and anus are on the underside. Here there are also five pairs of wavy grooves, which took food to the mouth. Living specimens have a fur-like covering of spines.

Size: This specimen is 89mm across
Distribution: North & South America, & West Indies
Time range: Tertiary to Quaternary

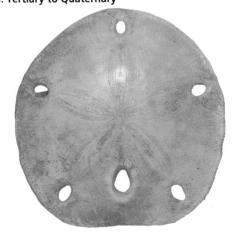

Sea Lilies & Starfish

Sea lilies look like plants, but are really animals. They have a root, a stem, and a flower-like structure called a 'calyx' (plural calices). The animal's delicate body is inside the calyx. Arms grow out from the calyx. They may be branched and have finer branches called 'pinnules'. These form a net for collecting food, which is then wafted into the mouth in the centre of the calyx. The stem is made of calcite plates called 'ossicles'. These vary in shape and may be round, star-shaped, or six-sided. The calyx is made of larger plates.

Macrocrinus

This sea lily specimen is of two calices, one with a length of stem. Pinnules form a feathery funnel around the mouth, which is deep in the centre of the small calyx. There are hair-like cilia on the pinnules, which would have wafted food toward the mouth. The ossicles on the stem become larger as they get farther away from the calyx.

Size: The larger specimen is 38mm long
Distribution: North America
Time range: Lower Carboniferous

Clematocrinus

A genus of small sea lilies. This specimen shows the calyx and arms with many slender branches. Only fragments of the stem have been preserved.

Size: This specimen is 25mm long
Distribution: North America, Europe, & Australia
Time range: Middle Silurian

Metopaster

This strange creature is an asteroid or starfish. It is related to the sea urchins and sea lilies. It has no arms. There is a five-sided outer wall of large plates, with many smaller plates within.

Size: Members of this genus grew to a maximum of 63mm across
Distribution: Europe – Time range: Cretaceous to Tertiary

Encrinus

This sea lily has a small calyx and well-developed arms. There are ten arms with many pinnules. The zigzag joins between the plates on the arms can be seen clearly. *Encrinus* lived in shallow, flowing sea water with its calyx facing the current. The densely packed pinnules sifted food from the water.

Size: This specimen is 38mm long
Distribution: Europe (but not UK), well known in Germany
Time range: Middle and Upper Triassic

Scyphocrinites

This specimen shows the calyx and branched arms of a sea lily which grew to over 1m long. The calyx is made of different kinds of plates. There are large ones at the base where it joins the stem. The plates of the upper part are smaller. At the base of the stem there is a bulbous structure. This may have been a float, enabling the sea lily to float in the sea currents.

Size: Area shown is 101mm long
Distribution: North America, north Africa, & Europe
Time range: Upper Silurian to Devonian

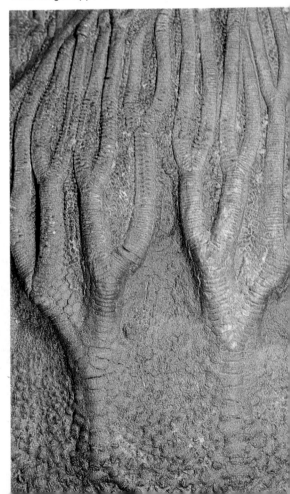

Palaeocoma

This is a genus of brittle stars. There is a central disk made of many small plates, and long snake-like arms. It is closely related to present-day brittle stars. When conditions were right, large numbers of these creatures were fossilized.

Size: Central disc up to 19mm across
Distribution: Europe – Time range: Jurassic to Cretaceous

Pentacrinites

The stem of this genus of sea lilies can be over 1m long. The stem ossicles are star-shaped. The small calyx has long arms with pinnules. Single fossils of *Pentacrinites* are often found in shales and limestones. Modern members of this genus live off the sea bed.

Size: Area shown is 19mm long
Distribution: North America & Europe
Time range: Triassic to Tertiary

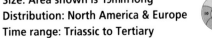

How Fossils Get There

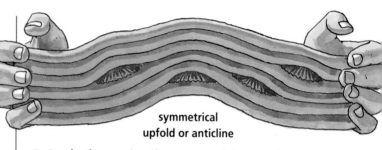

Fossils are found between layers of sedimentary rock called strata. These layers are being laid down all the time, today as well as in the past. They range from a fraction of a centimetre to several metres thick. Forces beneath the Earth's crust can fold and twist the layers. This can make it difficult to work out in what order the layers were laid down. It also pushes fossils to the surface, which would otherwise stay hidden deep below.

Find out about strata

You will need: several lengths of Play-doh in different colours, some small shells, and a table knife.

1 **Roll out the lengths of Play-doh** into strips that are long, flat, and about 3 cm wide. Make them different thicknesses.
2 **Lay one strip on top of another.** The top strip represents the sea bed. Each strip is a new layer of sediment.

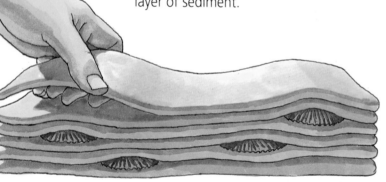

3 **Place a shell on to the 'sea bed'** on every second layer before laying down another strip. The shells are your fossils.
4 **Complete all the layers.** This is how an undisturbed section of sedimentary rock would look. The youngest layers are at the top.

symmetrical
upfold or anticline

5 **Push the ends of your model together.** This represents the movement of the Earth's crust.
6 **If you push equally hard at each end,** the strata will form a symmetrical upfold, or anticline. A symmetrical downfold, or syncline, may also happen.

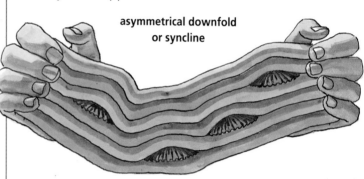

asymmetrical downfold
or syncline

7 **If you push harder at one end** than the other, an asymmetrical upfold or downfold may happen.

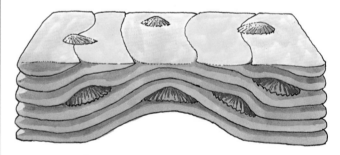

8 **Cut the top off of an anticline** with the knife. The knife represents weathering by wind or water, or quarrying by people.
9 **You can see that all the layers,** even the oldest, are now exposed. Fossils may be at, or just below, the surface.

Make your own fossil

You will need: Plasticine (Play-doh won't work), plaster of Paris, and a plastic container.

1 **Make a fossil shape** out of the Plasticine.
2 **Find an old plastic container** that is deep enough to take your fossil.

3 **Mix up enough plaster of Paris** to half-fill the container and pour it in. Before it sets, press your shell into the plaster.

4 **Roll out some Plasticine** into thin lengths. Use them to cover the surface of the plaster. Go right up to the edges of the container and mould them around the shell.

5 **Mix some more plaster of Paris** and pour it over the thin Plasticine layer. Make sure that it covers your fossil, and let it set.

6 **When the plaster is hard**, take it out and separate the two halves, and peel away the Plasticine. Remove the fossil shape. The two halves of the solid plaster now form a mould.

7 **Dust the inside of both halves** of the mould with talcum powder.

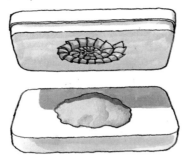

8 **Press a soft lump of self-hardening, modelling clay** into one half of the mould. Firmly press the other half of the mould on top.

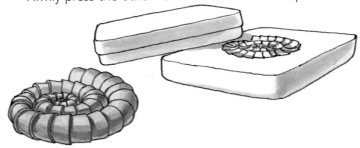

9 **Open the two halves of the mould**. Inside will be a cast 'fossil' (see page 8) of your original model. The modelling clay represents the minerals that replaced the material from which the original shell was made.

Molluscs: Bivalves

There are many different kinds of mollusc. Most of them have a shell protecting the outside of their soft bodies. Beneath the shell is a slippery outer skin, or mantle. The shape of the shell varies, depending on where the mollusc lives.

Bivalves are a kind of mollusc. They live in oceans, lakes, and ponds. Some are fixed to the bottom, others burrow, some can swim, and others move along the sea bed with the aid of a fleshy, tongue-like foot which pokes out of the shell. The shell is in two often identical parts, called 'valves'. These are hinged and can be opened and closed by a system of muscles. The pointed end of the shell is the front and is called the 'umbo' (plural umbones). Two 'siphons' (or tubes) also exit the shell. One sucks food into the mouth, the other removes waste. Bivalves are common fossils.

Dunbarella

These semi-circular bivalves have very pointed umbones. The hinge line is straight and there are wing-like flaps on either side of the umbones. The thin valves are marked by ribs spreading out from the umbo and faint growth lines.

Size: Up to 38mm across
Distribution: North America & Europe
Time range: Carboniferous

Schizodus

A group of oval-shaped bivalves with very faint ribs and growth lines. The umbones stick out. This specimen is a cast fossil – the original shell dissolved away, leaving a hollow space (see page 8). The fossil is made of sediment, which filled up the empty space. *Schizodus* lived on the slopes of reefs in deep water. It is found with sea lilies, brachiopods, corals, and trilobites.

Size: Up to 50mm long
Distribution: Worldwide
Time range: Carboniferous to Permian

Nuculana

Small bivalves with a triangular outline. The umbones are at the front and the shell is elongated toward the rear. Growth lines can be seen. *Nuculana* burrowed into the sea bed and poked siphons through to the surface. These brought food and oxygen into the shell and released waste back into the water.

Size: Up to .19mm long
Distribution: Worldwide
Time range: Triassic to Quaternary

Carbonicola

This group of bivalves lived in lakes and rivers at the time of the great Carboniferous forests. These are the forests which later became coal. The umbones face forward and the valves are stretched toward the rear end. There are lines on the shell which show the stages of growth. *Carbonicola* used a fleshy foot to move through the mud.

Size: Up to 63mm long
Distribution: Europe & CIS (formerly the USSR)
Time range: Upper Carboniferous

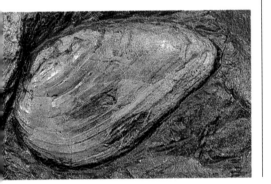

Oxytoma

Almost round bivalves, with one valve curving outward more than the other. There are wings on each side of the umbones. There may also be a large spine growing out from the umbones. The valves have several thick ribs. The shell may be extended where these reach the outer edge. There are finer ribs between the thick ones and faint growth lines.

Size: Up to 63mm long
Distribution: Worldwide
Time range: Upper Triassic to Upper Cretaceous

Anthraconauta

This photograph shows a large number of these bivalves preserved in shale. The thin shell is elongated and there are clear growth lines. They lived in streams and rivers surrounded by the vast Carboniferous forests.

Size: Up to 50mm long
Distribution: Europe & CIS
Time range: Carboniferous to Permian

Cardinia

The outline of these bivalves is oval or triangular. There are thick growth lines. The valves are thick and strong, which enabled the bivalve to survive being jostled and jolted in shallow seas. The specimen shown is an average size for one of these bivalve molluscs. Found in sandstones, shales, and mudstones with ammonites, other bivalves, gastropods, and belemnites.

Size: Up to 203mm long
Distribution: Worldwide
Time range: Upper Triassic to Lower Jurassic

Bivalves

Chlamys

The valves of these bivalves are not exactly identical. One is more domed than the other. They have round outer edges, but are straight at the hinge. The valves have spines which broke off before fossilization. There are large 'ears' on the umbones, one larger than the other. Some species of this genus were fixed to the sea bed by a mass of threads, called a 'byssus'. Others swam.

Size: Up to 101mm long – Distribution: Worldwide
Time range: Triassic to Quaternary

Lopha

A genus of oysters. *Lopha* has strong valves for surviving on the bed of choppy, shallow seas. The valves of this specimen have been separated. The inner surface (on the right) has a scar where a muscle was attached. One valve curves outward, the other inward, and they meet at a zigzag edge. There are thick ribs.

Size: Up to 120mm long
Distribution: Worldwide
Time range: Triassic to Cretaceous

Exogyra

Oysters have valves which are very different from each other. One is flat, the other curves outward. The shell is in a spiral shape with the umbones coiled toward the rear end. The outline of the outer edge is round, and the valve edges are toothed or notched. There is also a deep ridge on the shell. *Exogyra* lived firmly attached to the sea bed.

Size: Up to 203mm long
Distribution: Europe
Time range: Cretaceous

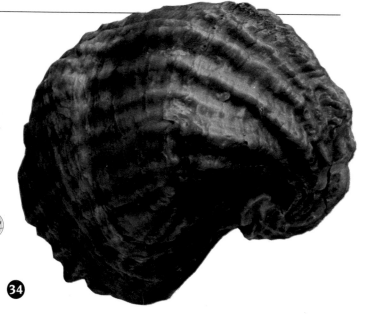

Plagistoma

Large bivalves with a shell marked faintly by ribs and growth lines. The outline is slightly triangular, although the edge of the rear end is rounded. At the front end, near the umbones, is a small wing-shaped piece. Both valves curve outward and are the same size. *Plagistoma* lived on or just below the sea bed, sometimes attached by a byssus.

Size: Up to 120mm across
Distribution: Worldwide
Time range: Triassic to Cretaceous

Myophorella

Bivalves with thick, curved valves and inward-pointing umbones. The valves have widely spaced rows of bumps which look like lengths of heavy rope. Each valve has one straight and one curved edge. This bivalve lived in shallow waters and burrowed a little way into the sea bed.

Size: Up to 101mm long
Distribution: Worldwide
Time range: Jurassic to Cretaceous

Camptonectes

A large bivalve with a rounded shell but a straight line at the hinge. The shell comes to a point at the umbones which have wings on each side. There are clear growth lines. *Camptonectes* was attached to the sea bed or other objects by byssal threads. They are found in sandstones and mudstones with other fossil bivalves, sea urchins, and brachiopods.

Size: Grew to 203mm across
Distribution: Worldwide
Time range: Lower Jurassic to Upper Cretaceous

Bivalves

Inoceramus

Broad ridges run across the valves of these bivalve molluscs. The overall shape of the shell is slightly oval, with long umbones. Both valves curve outward. *Inoceramus* was attached by byssal threads to the sea bed or floating material like wood. This specimen has some of its shell left. This shows as the white parts of the fossil.

Size: Up to 120mm long
Distribution: Worldwide
Time range: Jurassic to Cretaceous

Spondylus

These bivalves have a very symmetrical shell. The outer edge forms a half-circle. The umbones are small and pointed and at the tip of a triangular point. There are regularly spaced growth lines and strong ribs. The shell had spines which helped to anchor the bivalve to the soft sea bed. These usually break off before fossilization. You can just see the stumps where the spines were on this specimen.

Size: Up to 120mm long
Distribution: Worldwide
Time range: Jurassic to Quaternary

Venericardia

This is a group of large bivalves with thick shells. There are growth lines and wide ribs with grooves between them. The edges of the valves are notched. These bivalves lived in shallow burrows with the rear ends level with the sea bed's surface. They were well suited to life in choppy, shallow seas. They are found in sandstones with other bivalves, and gastropods like *Turritella* and *Natica*.

Size: Up to 152mm across
Distribution: North America, Africa, and Europe
Time range: Tertiary

Modiolus

These common bivalve fossils are relatives and ancestors of the present-day mussel, which is common on beaches. The thin shell is stretched out toward the rear end. The valves are the same size and straight where they are hinged. There are clear growth lines.

Size: Up to 101mm long
Distribution: Worldwide
Time range: Devonian to Quaternary

Pseudopecten

Members of this well-known bivalve group were able to swim by flapping their valves. Strong ribs spread out from pointed umbones to a rounded outside edge. The shell also has growth lines. Inside each valve is a single large scar where a muscle was attached.

Size: Up to 203mm across
Distribution: Europe, South America, & East Indies
Time range: Jurassic

Pholadomya

This bivalve group have very elongated shells. There is a 'gape' (or gap) between the valves at the rear end. This is common in bivalves that burrow. The gape allows the siphons to stick out to the surface of the sediment, even if the shell is in a tight hole. The valves have bold ribs and faint growth lines.

Size: Up to 120mm long
Distribution: Worldwide – Time range: Triassic to Quaternary

Gryphaea

Size: *G. arcuata* grew to about 165mm long;
G. giganteum grew to about 203mm across
Distribution: Worldwide
Time range: Upper Triassic to Upper Jurassic

A genus of oysters, of which two species are shown here. The valves are not the same. *Gryphaea arcuata* (above) has one large, heavy, and curved valve with hooked umbones. The other valve is flatter and curves inward. The larger valve has heavy growth lines. The umbones often lean to one side. *Gryphaea giganteum* (below) has a much wider and flatter shell with a rounded outline. Young specimens were fixed to the sea bed with byssal threads. Older oysters simply rested on the sea bed with the larger, curved valve underneath.

Trace Fossils

Living things do not only leave behind parts of themselves to become fossilized. They also leave behind tracks, trails, burrows and dung. These are known as trace fossils. These fossils tell us about prehistoric environments (what the countryside was like) and the way that ancient animals lived. Many creatures, including molluscs, worms, arthropods and dinosaurs, have left trace fossils.

The speed of dinosaurs

A series of fossilized footprints can be used to work out the speed of a walking or running dinosaur. The distance between the footprints is the stride. Some dinosaurs walked at between 4-8 Kilometres per hour (kph). Others could run at 40 kph. It is also possible to work out the dinosaur's height and weight, and whether it walked on two or four legs. A large animal takes long strides, while a small animal takes very small strides.

Walk like a dinosaur

You can stomp across a sandy beach leaving an alarming trail of dinosaur footprints. Here is the outline of a meat-eating dinosaur's footprint. The real one is about 30cm long and about 25cm wide with three toes and long claws.

1 **Draw this outline** (enlarged slightly if necessary) on to a piece of heavy cardboard or plywood. Do this twice.
2 **Cut out the cardboard,** or ask an adult to cut out the wood shapes for you.
3 **Drill four holes into each shape** and thread a length of string through the holes. Tie the shapes to your feet. Add longer strings for your hands to make walking easier.
4 **Notice how the size of the shapes** makes you swing your legs around.

Satapliasaurus

This is the footprint of a two-legged dinosaur which roamed muddy marshlands. It is a cast fossil which was found when the rock was split It is not possible to work out from a footprint exactly what the dinosaur looked like.

Sometimes large numbers of footprints of different sizes are found in one place. This shows us that the dinosaurs lived in a herd.

The specimen shown here is 15cm long, but some have been found up to 61cm long It is from the Middle Jurassic period.

Make a trace fossil

You will need: a tray of damp sand, a piece of cardboard about 5 x 38cm, plaster of Paris, water, and some paper clips.

1 **Smooth the sand until it is level.** Push your hand or foot firmly into the tray to make a print.

2 **Place the cardboard strip in a ring** around the print. Paper clip it together so that it is firm and push it a little way into the sand. It should form a raised border around the print.

3 **Mix up enough plaster of Paris** to fill the mould. Pour it into the cardboard circle and fill it to just below the brim. Leave the plaster to dry.

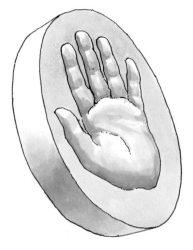

4 **When the plaster has set,** remove the cardboard strip. Lift the plaster out of the sand. You should have a cast of your hand or foot.

5 **Try making a cast of a 'burrow'** as well. Make the burrow by pushing a pencil or a pipe cleaner into the sand. Then pour in plaster of Paris.

Scolicia

This long, curved fossil shows the grazing trail of a gastropod mollusc (see pages 46–51). It is preserved as a cast. Minerals have filled in the grooved trail left on the sandy sea bed.

The area shown is 20cm across. Specimens have been found from all periods between the Cambrian and Quarternary

Coprolite

This is the fossil of a lump of turtle droppings. Such fossils can tell us what kind of food the turtle ate. Coprolite is the word used to describe larger droppings. The smaller droppings of arthropods and molluscs are called 'fecal pellets'. This specimen is covered in the iron mineral limonite.

This specimen is 32mm long It comes from North America and dates from the Tertiary Period

Cephalopods

This group of molluscs lived in the sea. They have shells which are divided up into chambers. Other molluscs do not have this feature. The ammonites and nautiloids have shells on the outside, which are usually coiled. The body is in the last chamber near the opening, and the front part of the body, with tentacles and eyes, sticks out of the shell. The other chambers, called 'buoyancy chambers', contain a mixture of gas and liquid. They raise the animal off the sea bed. Squids, cuttles, and belemnites have the shell inside their bodies.

Actinoceras

These early nautiloids have a straight, tube-shaped shell which is divided into chambers. There is a tube going from the body chamber to the buoyancy chambers. This is the 'siphuncle'. It is thought that cephalopods used this tube to alter the contents of the buoyancy chambers. They could control their depth in this way. This thin, broken specimen shows the chambered shell. The walls between the chambers are known as 'septa'.

Size: This specimen is 82mm long
Distribution: Worldwide
Time range: Lower Ordovician to Carboniferous

Nautilus

These large molluscs had a large, outer whorl, which partly hid the inner whorls. The cross-section of the fossil clearly shows the septa dividing the shell into chambers, and the siphuncle tube (see *Actinoceras*) passing through some of these chambers. A modern-day relative can be found in the western Pacific and northern Australia.

Size: Up to152mm across
Distribution: North America, Europe, Asia, & north Africa
Time range: Jurassic to Quaternary

Orthoceras

These extinct nautiloids have a long, slender shell which tapers, or narrows, to a point. The chambers are divided by septa. There are lines to show where the septa met the outside shell. These are called 'suture' lines.

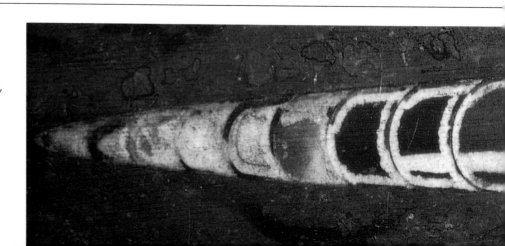

Clymenia

This early ammonoid group has a smooth, coiled shell. There are faint ribs. These spread out like spokes from the hub of a wheel. The 'hub' (or centre) of the ammonite shell is called the 'umbilicus'. *Clymenia*'s whorls are loosely held together, so they can all be seen clearly. In some ammonoids the outer whorl covers up the inner ones.

Size: Up to 82mm across
Distribution: Europe
Time range: Devonian

Prolecanites

Most of the whorls of this ammonoid can be seen. They are narrow and flattened. The outer shell of this specimen is missing. The wavy suture lines are clearly seen. These lines go right up to the the end of the last whorl, which means that the body chamber is missing.

Size: Up to 203mm across
Distribution: North America, Europe, & Asia
Time range: Carboniferous

Echioceras

This is an open-coiled group of ammonites in which all the whorls can be seen. There are thick, well-spaced ribs which spread out from the centre like the spokes of a wheel. A thin ridge runs around the outside edge (not shown). A species of this group, *Echioceras raricostatum*, is a zone fossil (see page 9) for part of the Lower Jurassic period.

Size: Up to 101mm across
Distribution: Worldwide
Time range: Lower Jurassic

Cladiscites

The outer whorl of these medium-sized ammonites hides the inner whorls completely. The umbilicus is very narrow. This specimen's shell has been worn down, and the delicate patterning of the suture lines can be seen. The body chamber is missing.

Size: Up to 203mm across
Distribution: Europe (but not UK), Alaska, & Himalayas
Time range: Triassic

They can only be seen when the outer shell has gone. *Orthoceras* swam near the sea bed with its tentacled body pointing down and buoyant shell rising above. Large numbers of these fossils form *Orthoceras* limestone. The long shells are often broken.

Size: The shell can be up to 4.8-5.2m long
Distribution: Worldwide
Time range: Lower Ordovician to Triassic

Ammonites

Pleuroceras

The inner whorls of these ammonites can clearly be seen. In cross-section the whorls are rectangular. The shell has thick, well-spaced ribs, which sometimes have spines and lumps near the outside edge. These are broken off in fossils. Some of the shell has been lost from this specimen. Suture lines can be seen on the whorls.

Size: Up to 101mm across
Distribution: Europe & north Africa
Time range: Lower Jurassic

Promicroceras

This is a genus of small ammonites with all their whorls showing. The shell is patterned with thick ribs that spread out from a wide umbilicus. They curve and become flat as they reach the outer edge. This specimen is crowded with fossils. Some have a complete shell, others do not. Suture lines can be seen where the shell is missing.

Size: Grew to a maximum of 38mm across
Distribution: Europe – Time range: Jurassic

Hildoceras

This specimen is a species called *Hildoceras bifrons*. It is a zone fossil (see page 9) for part of the Lower Jurassic period. Most of the inner whorls are showing and the ribs are curved. Many of these fossils are found in dark shale cliffs in Whitby, North Yorkshire, UK. They are named after St. Hilda, who founded the abbey there.

Size: Up to 120mm across
Distribution: Europe, Asia Minor, & Japan
Time range: Lower Jurassic

Asteroceras

A group of ammonites patterned with thick, widely spaced ribs. These curve forward as they reach the outside edge. In this specimen, the buoyancy chambers are filled with pale calcite. Fossils of this family are commonly found with bivalves, such as *Gryphaea*, *Pholadomya*, and *Pseudopecten*. In the same rocks sea lilies, including *Pentacrinites*, brachiopods, and trace fossil burrows (see page 39,) can be found.

Size: Up to 101mm across
Distribution: North America, Europe, & Asia
Time range: Lower Jurassic

Dactylioceras

An ammonite group with all their whorls showing.
Cut through, each whorl is rounded in section.
There are thick ribs which split into two as they go
across the outer edge. Some species have rows of
lumps on the inner whorls.

Size: Up to 101mm across
Distribution: Worldwide – Time range: Lower Jurassic

Lytoceras

A group of loosely coiled ammonites with all whorls
showing. The whorls are round in cross-section,
getting larger toward the opening. The shell is
patterned with fine ribs, which are slightly wavy at
the edges of the whorls. There may be stronger ribs
near the opening.

Size: Up to 152mm across
Distribution: Worldwide
Time range: Jurassic

Amaltheus

This group of ammonites has a
flattened shell and hidden inner
whorls. In this specimen there is
sediment in the centre. The ribs
curve forward as they reach the
outside edge on which there is a
ridge. This is ribbed like a length
of heavy rope. These ammonites
are found in different kinds of
sedimentary rock, including
limestones and sandstones.

Size: Up to 82mm across
Distribution: North America,
Europe, north Africa, & Asia
Time range: Lower Jurassic

Psiloceras

This is an important fossil group. *Psiloceras
planorbis* is a zone fossil (see page 9) for the oldest
zone of the Jurassic Period. Usually the fossils have
been crushed flat in layers of shale, but this
specimen shows three-dimensional examples. Part
of the body chamber can be seen – it has no
suture lines.

Size: Up to 70mm across
Distribution: North & South America, Europe, north
Africa, and Indonesia – Time range: Lower Jurassic

Ammonites

In some genera of ammonites the males and females have shells of different sizes. It is not possible, however, to tell from just the shells which is male and which is female. The smaller of the two is called the 'microconch', and the larger one is called the 'macroconch'.

Acanthoscaphites

These ammonites have a slight uncoiling of the outside whorl. The inner whorls are hidden. The shell is flattened and broad. There are closely spaced ribs which curve near the centre. There are swellings here. The opening is slightly hooked and faces the rest of the shell.

Size: Up to 50mm across
Distribution:
North America, Europe, South Africa, Australia, & Chile
Time range:
Cretaceous

Quenstedtoceras

The males and females in this genus of ammonites also have shells of different sizes. Two specimens of the microconch are shown. The one below shows the buoyancy chambers inside. The inner whorls are partially hidden. There are strong, curved ribs which split into two. They form a chevron (or V-shaped) pattern on the outside edge. The macroconch shells have less patterning.

Size: Microconch up to 63mm; Macroconch up to 177mm
Distribution: Worldwide
Time range: Middle and Upper Jurassic

Kosmoceras

In this genus of ammonites the males and females have shells of different sizes. The microconch, shown here, has a long piece of shell growing from the opening. This is called a lappet. The shell also has spines and lumps.

Size: Microconch up to 63mm across
Distribution: Worldwide
Time range: Middle Jurassic

Cardioceras

Again, in this genus of ammonites the males and females have shells of different sizes. Only part of the inner whorls is visible. The main ribs split into two before they reach the outside edge. The microconch has an extra piece at the opening called a 'rostrum'. The macroconch does not have this extra piece.

Size: Microconch, 63mm across; Macroconch, 127mm across
Distribution: Worldwide – **Time range:** Upper Jurassic

Parkinsonia

These common ammonites look rather like *Dactylioceras* (see page 43), even though they lived millions of years apart. The whorls are all visible. The shell is patterned with ribs which split into two on the outside edge. There is a slight groove running around the outside edge, which the ribs do not cross – *Dactylioceras* does not have this ridge.

Size: Up to 152mm across
Distribution: Europe, Asia, north Africa, & Iran
Time range: Middle Jurassic

Mantelliceras

Only part of the inner whorls show in this ammonite group. There are thick ribs which develop two rows of lumps where they cross the outside edge. These fossils are often found with other ammonites, and bivalves like *Chlamys*, *Inoceramus*, *Exogyra*, and *Lopha*. The echinoid *Holaster* is also often found with them.

Size: Up to 101mm across
Distribution: US, Europe, north Africa, India, & southeast Asia
Time range: Cretaceous

Turrilites

An ammonite group with a strangely shaped shell. It is coiled into a spiral like a gastropod. Unlike gastropods, however, *Turrilites* has suture lines and chambers. There are weak ribs and well-formed swellings. It probably swam with the buoyant shell on top and its tentacled body facing the sea bed.

Size: Up to 152mm long
Distribution: Worldwide
Time range: Cretaceous

Baculites

These ammonites have a very small, coiled shell in the early stages of life. It then uncoils. The shell is often broken and only short pieces are found as fossils. This specimen shows the fine and intricate suture lines, which help to identify it as an ammonite. Sometimes there are also ribs and swellings. There is a rostrum on one side of the opening.

Size: Up to 2m long
Distribution: Worldwide
Time range: Upper Cretaceous

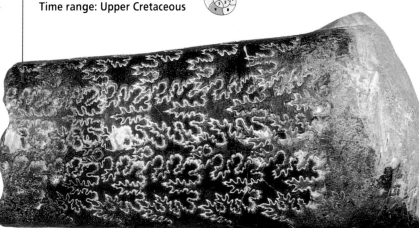

Gastropods & Others

Dentalium

This fossil belongs to a class of molluscs called the scaphopods. Three different species are shown in this photograph. They are all tube-shaped and usually have ribs running from top to bottom. Present-day scaphopods live in the sea bed with the narrow end poking up into the water. Sea water is sucked in and pushed out at this end. From the other end the foot and many thin arms covered with cilia stick out.

Size: Up to 63mm long – Distribution: Worldwide
Time range: Silurian to Quaternary

Belemnitella

This is a common group of belemnites. The surface of the fossil is marked with lines and grooves. These spread apart at the pointed apex. Complete specimens may have a larger, chambered section. This is joined to the wider end of the guard. These fossils are difficult to collect because they break easily.

Size: These specimens are about 101mm long
Distribution: North America, Europe, Asia, & Greenland
Time range: Upper Cretaceous

Acrocoelites

These animals are called belemnites – squid-like creatures which had tentacles and eyes. They are cephalopods, like the ammonites. They belong to a class which includes squids, octopods, and cuttles. The fossils are bullet-shaped and are the 'guard' (or inside shell). The photograph shows a mass of fossils all lying the same way. They may have been swept into this arrangement by a strong current.

Size: Up to 120mm long
Distribution: Europe and North America
Time range: Lower Jurassic

Present-day gastropods include snails, slugs, limpets, and whelks. Most have an outside shell which is coiled in a spiral. The body of the animal is in the last, and usually largest, whorl, next to the opening. The animal poked its head and fleshy foot out of this opening. There is sometimes a groove on the opening, called the 'siphonal notch', which drew water to the gills. Gastropods live in fresh water, at sea, and on land.

Poleumita

The coiled shell of these gastropods has a flattened upper surface. In the centre of each whorl is a prominent ridge. The shell is marked by fine lines which spread out across the shell from the centre. There may also be small spines. *Poleumita* is found in sediments laid down in shallow sea water.

Size: Up to 63mm across
Distribution: North America and Europe – Time range: Silurian

Straparollus

Gastropods with a coiled shell, which may be a high spiral or flat. The shell is smooth, but has many thin ribs spreading out across the whorls. There is a slight flat-topped ridge running along the centre of each whorl. These fossils are preserved in limestones formed in shallow seawater and on the slopes of reefs.

Size: Up to 50mm cross
Distribution: Worldwide – Time range: Silurian to Permian

Mourlonia

These gastropods have a spire-shaped shell that ends in a narrow, rounded point, or 'apex'. The whorls get wider and flatter toward the opening. The sutures (or joining lines) between the whorls are thin. The shell has a pattern of thin spiralling ribs. *Mourlonia* crawled on the sea bed in very shallow water.

Size: Up to 38mm across
Distribution: Worldwide
Time range: Ordovician to Permian

Gastropods

Conotomaria

These cone-shaped fossils have whorls which have only shallow sutures between them. The base of the shell is flat. The shell is marked with spiralling lines and low ridges. This specimen is an internal cast fossil (see page 8). *Conotomaria* lived and crawled on the sea bed. It is found with other fossils, including bivalves and ammonites.

Size: Up to 152mm tall
Distribution: Worldwide
Time range: Middle Jurassic to Tertiary

Ficus

Ficus is a pear-shaped gastropod with a large body whorl. This whorl covers most of the other whorls; only the pointed apex sticks out. At the other end, the opening also tapers to a narrow base. The shell is marked by squiggly lines. *Ficus* lived in shallow seas, and is often fossilized with other gastropods like *Turritella*.

Size: Up to 101mm long
Distribution: Worldwide – Time range: Tertiary to Quaternary

Bourguetia

These sea snails lived in shallow seas, and were quite large gastropods. They have large, heavy shells which taper to a blunt apex. The whorls are smooth, although there may be thin growth lines. This specimen has many small, round marks on the shell. These were made by ooliths, grains of the oolitic limestone in which the shell was preserved.

Size: Up to 101mm long
Distribution: Europe
Time range: Middle & Upper Jurassic

Pleurotomaria

This group of sea-living gastropods are often preserved with ammonites, belemnites, bivalves, brachiopods, and corals. The whorls are coiled in a low spiral. They get larger.toward the opening, which is large and flares out. The shell is marked with growth lines, lumps, and bands. There are deep grooves, or 'sutures', between the whorls.

Size: Up to 120mm tall – Distribution: Worldwide
Time range: Jurassic to Cretaceous

Cerithium

These gastropods have a long, slender, cone-shaped shell with many small whorls. Each whorl has a ridge covered with small spines and lumps. There are spiralling growth lines which form an S-shape on the final body whorl. The small opening is pear-shaped. These specimens have been preserved in clay formed on the seabed.

Size: Up to 31mm long
Distribution: Worldwide
Time range: Upper Cretaceous to Quaternary

Rimella

This is a group of sea-living gastropods with cornet-shaped shells. The spire tapers to a point. The opening has a long siphonal canal that stretches to the apex. This is on the underside of the specimen shown. The shell has a pattern of curved ribs.

Size: Up to 31mm long
Distribution:
Worldwide
Time range:
Upper Cretaceous
to Quaternary

Sycostoma

These sea-living gastropods have a large, tapering body whorl. This is followed by the other whorls forming a cone. They end in a rounded apex. There is a slight ridge following each suture. The surface of the shell is marked by ribs and thin, encircling lines.

Size: Grew to a height of about 70mm
Distribution: Worldwide
Time range: Upper Cretaceous to Tertiary

Gastropods

Ancilla

These gastropods have a smooth shell with thin sutures. The body whorl is much larger than the others, which end in a sharp apex. The opening is large and there is a wide siphonal notch. These are on the underside of the specimen shown. The surface of the shell remains shiny only if preservation is very good.

Size: Up to 50mm long
Distribution:
Worldwide
Time range:
Upper Cretaceous
to Quaternary

Natica

These gastropods killed and ate other shellfish. They softened their shells with acid, then drilled a hole through to the soft body inside. *Natica's* shell is thick and dome-shaped. The body whorl is very large. Its outer wall overlaps the other whorls. There was an 'operculum' (or lid) covering the opening, which is often missing in fossils.

Size: Up to 31mm tall
Distribution:
Worldwide
Time range:
Cretaceous
to Quaternary

Planorbis

Planorbis has a small, round shell which curves inward on one side and is flatter on the other. It looks like an ammonite, except that ammonites curve inward on both sides. This fossil has a smooth surface with faint growth lines. Present-day members of this group live in still and running fresh water. They feed on algae and other plants. Some species breathe using a simple lung.

Size: Up to 31mm across – Distribution: Worldwide
Time range: Tertiary to Quaternary

Crucibulum

This fossil belongs to a genus of gastropods known as 'slipper limpets'. The thick shell is pyramid-shaped and completely open at the base. Modern members of this group begin life as males and turn into females after three years. They then become less active and stick themselves to dead shells or rocks.

Size: Up to 50mm tall
Distribution: North America,
West Indies, & Europe
Time range: Tertiary to Quaternary

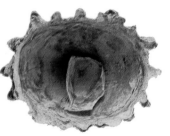

Turritella

Gastropods with a long, narrow, screw-shaped shell. The whorls overlap slightly and there are deep sutures between them. The opening is almost square in shape. The shell is patterned with growth lines which spiral around it. Present-day members of this group burrow into the sea bed with the apex pointing down. The opening is held just above the surface of the sediment.

Size: Up to 50mm long
Distribution: Worldwide – Time range: Tertiary to Quaternary

Volutospina

An average-sized gastropod, where the large body whorl tapers to a narrow base, and the other whorls spiral to a point. There are strong ribs and growth lines. The whorls have ridges, or shoulders, which are covered with pointed bumps.

Size: Up to 120mm long
Distribution: Worldwide
Time range: Upper Cretaceous to Quaternary

Conus

Species of *Conus* have a shell which tapers to a point at both ends. There is a large body whorl and a long, narrow opening. The other whorls form a pyramid-shape. There are growth lines with bumps running around the shell. The group is often fossilized in great numbers, as shown here. Today, this group lives in warm seas, like the Mediterranean.

Size: Up to 120mm long
Distribution: Worldwide
Time range: Upper Cretaceous to Quaternary

Housing Your Collection

A collection of fossils is more enjoyable and more valuable to science if it is well organized. It is good to see the results of your hard work on display, and it is useful to be able to call up information about the specimens quickly.

You might like to keep a diary recording when and where you find your fossils. Take your field notebook with you when you go fossil hunting. Make sketches of the area and fossils for your diary.

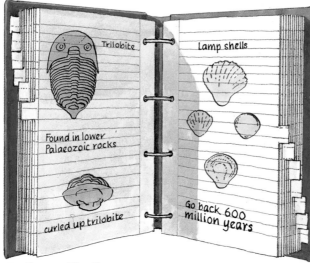

Trilobite

Found in lower Palaeozoic rocks

curled up trilobite

Lamp shells

Go back 600 million years

A fossil diary

Keep your diary in a looseleaf binder on separate sheets of paper. Fill out a sheet for each fossil-hunting trip you go on with the details from your field notebook. You can also write notes in it when you visit museums, or see a television program about fossils. You can decorate it with your own drawings, photographs, pictures from magazines, postcards, and so on.

You will need: large sheets of coloured card, a ruler, a pencil, a pair of scissors, a felt-tip pen.

1 **Cut the sheets of card into 12 pages** that are the same height as your paper, but 1cm wider than the paper.

Organizing your collection

You may want to put special or delicate specimens in a glass-fronted cabinet. This will protect them from damage and dust. The rest of your collection can be kept in individual trays in a drawer or shallow box.

1 **Number each fossil and keep a card index file** with information about them. The numbers on the cards should correspond with the numbers on the fossils. This will make it easy to look up the information.

2 **Put a small patch of correcting fluid** on to an unimportant part of each fossil. Then carefully write on the fossil's number.

2 **Divide the height of the cardboard pages** into twelve. On the first page cut away $^{11}/_{12}$ths of the 1cm margin, leaving the last twelfth at the top to form a tag.

3 **On the second card page**, cut away $^{11}/_{12}$ths of the margin, but this time leave the tag $^{1}/_{12}$th down from the top.

4 **Repeat this ten times**, each time leaving the tag in a different position.

5 **Write one of the twelve months of the year** on to each of the twelve tags. When you put these card pages into your file, they will act as dividers. If you have positioned the tags in the right way, they should not overlap.

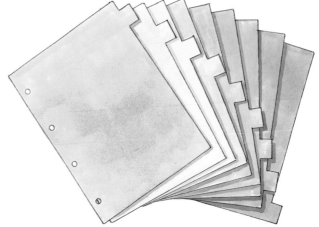

3 **If you make trays for your fossils** (see opposite page), you can adjust the dividers to fit the specimens. Or you can re-use the Styrofoam trays from grocery stores used to pack eggs.

4 **Line each tray with cotton** for added protection and place a small label card in each one. This could just say the name of the fossil, its number, and where it was found.

Keeping a record

Your card index file should give detailed information about each fossil, like:

- the fossil's number
- its name, if known, or the group to which it belongs
- the date it was found
- where it was found: name and description of place, and map references
- type of rock in which it was found
- recognizable features nearby, like a cave or a hill
- the weather on the day of your visit

You may be able to store your information on a computer. Keep an up-to-date print-out, as well as your disk and its back-up.

A home for your collection

You will need: some shoe boxes (with lids) and some stiff card. If you don't have any shoe boxes at home, visit the local shoe shop and ask if you can have some.

1 **Measure the box** across its short side and its depth. Draw a rectangle **(A)** on the card to match (e.g. 15 x 12 cm). Draw two lines across the rectangle to divide it into three.

2 **Measure the long side** (e.g. 30 x 12cm). Draw another rectangle **(B)** to match this size. Draw two lines across it to divide it into three.

3 **Cut out each rectangle**; then cut another one each of **(B)** and **(A)**, using the first rectangles as patterns. You could have extra partitions.

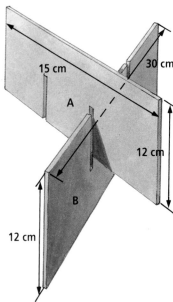

4 **Pad the bottom of the box** with cotton if you like. Then cut halfway up each dividing line of each partition and slot them together as shown. Last, slide the partitions into the box.

5 **Paint the boxes and their lids** with emulsion paint so that they match.

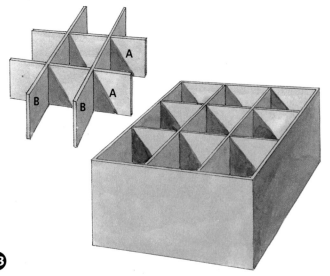

Arthropods

Trilobites belong to a large phylum of animals known as the arthropods. Today this group includes spiders and insects, scorpions, crabs, and lobsters. The trilobites lived through a timespan of 300 million years, but then became extinct. We know them only from their fossils.

The trilobite's 'exoskeleton' (or outside shell), was made of jointed segments. To grow, the animal had to moult (shed) this exoskeleton. One trilobite could therefore leave behind more than one fossil. Trilobites' exoskeletons are in three sections: the head-shield, or 'cephalon', the tail-shield, or 'pygidium'; and a middle section, called the 'thorax'. From head to tail the body is also divided into three lobes (or sections). The middle lobe is called the 'axis'. They all lived in the sea.

Ogygopsis

This group of trilobites has a long, deeply furrowed glabella in the centre of the head-shield. There are many thoracic segments. The axis tapers toward the pygidium, which is larger than the cephalon and has a narrow border around it. Short genal spines (see *Olenellus*) are present in undamaged fossils.

Size: Up to 101mm long
Distribution: North America – Time range: Cambrian

Ogyginus

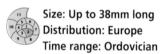
Size: Up to 38mm long
Distribution: Europe
Time range: Ordovician

The cephalon and pygidium of this trilobite group are the same size. There is a large glabella with oval-shaped eyes either side of it. Genal spines extend a short way along the thorax. These are often broken off, but can be seen here. The thoracic axis continues to the pygidium, then tapers rapidly. There are eight thoracic segments.

Olenellus

These medium-sized trilobites have a wide cephalon and a furrowed glabella. There are large, crescent-shaped eyes at the edge of the glabella. The thoracic axis narrows to a point and becomes a tail-spine. The thoracic segments have spines and there are two spines on the cephalon, which are called 'genal' spines.

Size: Up to 82mm long
Distribution: North America, Greenland, & northern Scotland
Time range: Cambrian

Elrathia

These trilobites have a cephalon that is wider than the thorax. There are two short genal spines (see *Olenellus*) on the cephalon and a short, oval-shaped glabella. The eyes are beside the glabella and sometimes joined to it by small ridges. The thoracic axis narrows toward the small pygidium. There are thirteen thoracic segments.

Size: Up to 31mm long
Distribution: North America
Time range: Cambrian

Peronopsis

This is a group of very small trilobites. They have only two thoracic segments. The cephalon and pygidium are the same size and have borders. The cephalon has a central glabella with a single furrow. *Peronopsis* is very similar to *Agnostus*, except that *Agnostus* has two small spines on its pygidium.

Size: Up to 6mm long
Distribution: North America, Europe, & Siberia
Time range: Cambrian

Trinucleus

Small trilobites with a large cephalon and a lump on the front of the glabella. The cephalon has a wide border with grooves. There are long genal spines, which stretch past the six thoracic segments to the pygidium. This is short and wide. *Trinucleus* is found in fine-grained sediment formed in deep seas, and is often found with the trilobite called *Ogygiocarella* (see page 56).

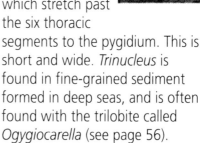

Size: Up to 31mm long
Distribution: Britain & CIS (formerly the USSR)
Time range: Ordovician

Paradoxides

One of the largest trilobites, *Paradoxides* had a thorax of over fifteen segments. These segments have ribs on the outer surface that often narrow to a point, and may have spines. The pygidium is small. The middle section of the head, called the 'glabella', is large and there are curved eyes.

Size: Up to 508mm long
Distribution: Europe, North & South America, Turkey, & north Africa
Time range: Cambrian

Trilobites

Phacops

Trilobites with many small lumps on the cephalon and thoracic axis. There are large kidney-shaped eyes. The thorax has eleven segments and the axis narrows only slightly before reaching the pygidium, where it then narrows rapidly. Commonly found in mudstones, shales and sandstones, fossils of this trilobite are often found in a rolled-up state.

Size: Up to 63mm long
Distribution: North America, Europe, & north Africa
Time range: Silurian to Devonian

Calymene

Two specimens of this trilobite are shown. One shows the trilobite curled up. Most trilobites were able to do this. It may have been a form of defence as used by present-day woodlice. The triangular cephalon has a large glabella, which has four rounded bumps. The thorax has twelve segments. The axis goes on to the pygidium, which has six segments.

Size: Up to 101mm long
Distribution: North & South America, Australia, & Europe
Time range: Silurian to Devonian

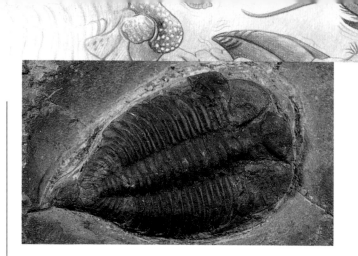

Dalmanites

These trilobites have a large, semicircular cephalon with genal spines. There are large eyes on the edge of the glabella. It is thought that these gave the animal good all-around vision, which is important for active swimmers. The small pygidium has a long tail-spine. There is also a spine on the cephalon. This may have supported the animal on the sea bed, or have been used for stirring up the sediment to find food.

Size: Up to 82mm long
Distribution: North America, Europe, CIS, & Australia
Time range: Silurian to Devonian

Ogygiocarella

This trilobite may also be seen in books and displays under the name of *Ogigia* or *Ogigiocaris*. It has a broad cephalon with long genal spines. The glabella reaches to the edge of the cephalon and there are crescent-shaped eyes. The thorax has eight segments. The axis hardly narrows at all at the thorax, but then narrows rapidly at the pygidium.

Size: Up to 82mm long
Distribution: Europe & South America
Time range: Ordovician

Triarthrus

Specimens of *Triarthrus* with preserved soft parts have been found in North America. These parts include antennae, and walking and gill-bearing limbs. The thorax has 12–16 segments. The small, triangular pygidium has five segments. The cephalon is semicircular with wide borders. The glabella is segmented and there are very small eyes.

Size: Up to 31mm long
Distribution: Worldwide
Time range: Ordovician

Illaenus

This is a group of trilobites, which have a cephalon and pygidium (see page 54) of the same size. Both are smooth, broad, and semicircular. The pygidium has no segments, but a deep groove, which follows the outline of the exo-skeleton. The glabella is not easy to see, but there are large, crescent-shaped eyes. The thorax has ten segments.

Size: Up to 50mm long
Distribution: Worldwide
Time range: Ordovician

Bumastus

Species of *Bumastus* have a short thorax with ten segments. The cephalon and pygidium are large, rounded, and smooth. The eyes are far over to the side of the glabella, which is hard to see clearly. This trilobite is sometimes found rolled up. It is found in limestones formed in shallow waters with corals, crinoids, brachiopods, and molluscs.

Size: Up to 101mm long
Distribution: North America & Europe
Time range: Silurian

Trimerus

Trilobites with an unusual thorax because there are no clear lobes. The axis is wide and the segments smooth. The pygidium is triangular and has an axis, which narrows to a point. There are no eyes. These points make scientists think that *Trimerus* may have been a burrower.

Size: Up to 203mm long
Distribution: Worldwide
Time range: Silurian to Devonian

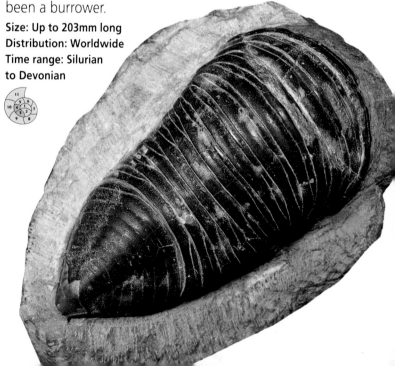

Other Arthropods

Pterygotus

This slender, scorpion-like creature lived in ancient seas and brackish water. Its body is segmented. The thorax narrows to a tail, which may have had spines. From the cephalon (see page 54) grow limbs carrying large, strong claws. There are also three pairs of paddle-shaped limbs and large eyes, which suggest they were probably fast-moving hunters.

Size: Up to 2m long
Distribution: North & South America, Europe, Asia, & Australia
Time range: Ordovician to Devonian

Mesolimulus

This is an ancestor of the king crabs, which live today. The cephalon is large and semicircular and has genal spines. The thorax is short and triangular, and the pygidium ends in a long tail-spine. There are five pairs of walking limbs and one pair of pincers. Present-day king crabs swim with the 'shell' below and the legs above. *Mesolimulus* probably swam in the same way.

Size: Up to 254mm long
Distribution: Europe
Time range: Triassic to Cretaceous

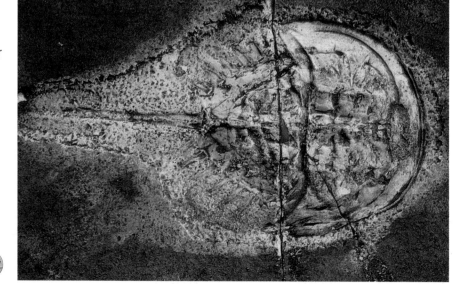

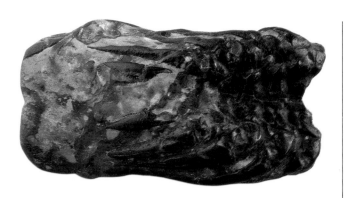

Hoploparia

These extinct lobsters have many points of similarity with present-day lobsters. The segmented shell has slender, pointed limbs. Both the specimens shown here are incomplete and were preserved in iron-rich rock.

Size: Larger specimen is 63mm long
Distribution: Worldwide
Time range: Tertiary

Euestheria

The 'carapace' (or shell) of this creature looks like that of a bivalve mollusc. In fact, this animal is a crustacean, belonging to a class known as Branchiopoda. The carapace is marked by growth lines, which were left by moulting. *Euestheria* lived in fresh water.

Size: Up to 12mm long – Distribution: Worldwide
Time range: Triassic to Jurassic

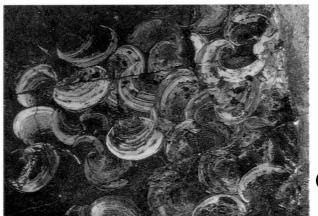

Libellula

This is the delicate fossil of a dragonfly larva (the second stage of its life cycle). It is preserved in very fine-grained limestone. This only happens when the soft sediment is laid down quickly in gentle conditions. The larva lives in water, and so is more likely to be preserved than the adult.

Size: This specimen is 12mm long
Distribution: Worldwide
Time range: Triassic to Quaternary

Glyphea

Members of the order that includes lobsters and shrimps, *Glyphea* has five pairs of limbs, which are not often preserved. The carapace is rough with a surface that is covered with small pits. The head has eyes and feelers. As it is often found with trace fossils of burrows known as *Thalassinoides* (see page 39), it is thought that *Glyphea* may have made these burrows.

Size: Up to 44mm long
Distribution: North America, Europe, Greenland, East Africa, & Australia
Time range: Triassic to Cretaceous

Brachipods

These are sea-living creatures with shells made up of two valves. Unlike bivalves, however, the valves are not the same size. The 'pedicle valve' is the larger of the two and has a hole in it. Living brachiopods have a fleshy stalk, called a pedicle, which sticks out of this hole and fixes the animal to the sea bed or to the base of a burrow. The smaller valve is called the 'brachial valve'. Brachiopods are still found in oceans today.

Lingula

This is a group of 'inarticulate' brachiopods, which means that they could not move their valves. The outline of the shell is oval and the valves are patterned with many thin ribs and growth lines. *Lingula* burrowed into the sea bed and had a pedicle as long as the shell. This is one of the longest surviving groups of brachiopods.

Size: Up to about 31mm long
Distribution: Worldwide
Time range: Ordovician to Quaternary

Leptaena

Articulate brachiopods (meaning they could open and close their valves) with a semicircular outline. The valves are straight where they are hinged. The pedicle valve curves outward, the brachial valve is flat. *Leptaena* lay on the sea floor with the brachial valve uppermost.

Size: Up to 50mm wide
Distribution: Worldwide
Time range: Ordovician to Devonian

Schizophoria

This group of articulate brachiopods has an almost oblong outline. Both valves curve outward, but the brachial valve curves more. Both are shown; the pedicle valve is on the left.

Size: Up to 50mm wide
Distribution: Worldwide
Time range: Silurian to Permian

Spirifer

These largish, articulate brachiopods have a semicircular outline with a straight hinge line which is the widest part. The umbo of the pedicle valve can be seen sticking up above the hinge line. The valves have bold ribs and growth lines. There is a fold on the brachial valve (facing us) which runs from the umbo (see page 32) to the edge.

Size: Up to 120mm wide
Distribution: Worldwide
Time range: Carboniferous

Pustula

These articulate brachiopods are almost oblong in outline and have a straight hinge line. The umbo on each valve is small and pointed. There are faint ribs, and growth lines which follow the outline of the shell. The pedicle valve (facing us) curves outward, the brachial valve is flat.

Size: Up to 120mm wide
Distribution: Europe
Time range: Carboniferous

Productus

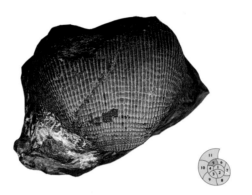

This genus of articulate brachiopods lay on the sea bed, with their brachial valves uppermost. The pedicle valve curves outward, the brachial valve is flat or curves inward. There are wavy growth lines on the surface. The shell once had spines which attached it to the sea bed, but these are usually broken off in fossils.

Size: Up to 30mm wide
Distribution: Europe & Asia
Time range: Carboniferous

Tetrarhynchia

Large numbers of these articulate brachiopods are often found preserved together in 'nests'. Both valves curve outward and are patterned with strong ribs. They meet at a zigzag fold. The umbones are small, pointed, and curved.

Size: Up to 19mm wide
Distribution: North America & Europe
Time range: Jurassic

Cyclothyris

These are articulate brachiopods, (meaning that they can open and close their valves). They are triangular in shape. Both valves curve outward and are patterned with ribs and growth lines. The brachial valve has a fold, and the valves meet at a zigzag line. There is a small pedicle opening – you can see it at the bottom of the right-hand specimen.

Size: Up to 31mm wide
Distribution: North America & Europe
Time range: Cretaceous

Terebratella

In the photograph of this articulate brachiopod, the brachial valve is facing us. The pedicle valve sticks out beyond it, and you can see the pedicle opening. The valves are patterned with ribs, which spread out from the umbo. Some of them divide into two. There are also growth lines.

Size: Up to 30mm long
Distribution: Worldwide
Time range: Jurassic to Quaternary

Plectothyris

These articulate brachiopods have a rounded shell edge, but it is triangular near the umbones. The pedicle opening is large. There are ribs only at the edge of the shell which is smooth elsewhere. These ribs started to develop only as the animal grew older. *Plectothyris* lived fixed to the sea bed alone or in groups.

Size: Up to 30mm wide
Distribution: Britain
Time range: Jurassic

Pygope

These articulate brachiopods were triangular. On the brachial valve there is a groove in the centre which develops into a hole. The animal squirted water out of its shell through this hole. This water was sucked into the shell through holes in the side so that the animal could extract food and oxygen from it. *Pygope* was fixed to the sea bed by its pedicle, which grew out of a large opening.

Size: Up to 82mm long
Distribution: Europe
Time range: Cretaceous

Graptolites

These strange, sea-living creatures are now extinct. They lived in colonies, but the animals themselves lived in cups, called 'thecae'. These were arranged on branching structures called 'rhabdosomes'. A single branch of these structures is known as a 'stipe'. Early graptolites lived on the sea bed, but later forms drifted in the sea currents.

Dictyonema

These are early graptolites. The rhabdosome is made up of many branches. When alive, this formed a cone-shaped net. The branches were joined together by web-like growths.

Size: Between 19 & 254mm long
Distribution: Worldwide
Time range: Cambrian to Carboniferous

Didymograptus

These graptolites are made up of two stipes joined together in a V-shape. The thecae are tube-shaped and on only one side of the stipe. *Didymograptus* drifted in sea currents. Fossils of it are sometimes found in great numbers, especially in shales and mudstones. They are delicate and found only in rocks with very fine grains.

Size: Between 19 & 609mm long
Distribution: Worldwide
Time range: Ordovician

Phyllograptus

These graptolites were made up of four stipes which looked like leaves. These are usually preserved alone or in pairs. The thecae were tube-shaped and faced upward. Fossils of *Phyllograptus* are often found in black shales. The photograph shows the fossil of a single stipe.

Size: Up to 19mm long – Distribution: Worldwide
Time range: Lower Ordovician

Climacograptus

These graptolites have S-shaped thecae with openings that face upward. They are arranged on both sides of a single stipe. It is thought to have drifted in the sea currents in an upright position.

Size: This specimen is 19mm long
Distribution: Worldwide
Time range: Ordovician
to Silurian

Monograptus

Graptolite with a single stipe which is usually straight, but may be curved or coiled. The thecae are arranged on one side of the stipe only and vary in shape. In some species they are simple cups, in others they are hook-shaped or S-shaped. This is a zone fossil (see page 9) for Silurian layers in the US, Great Britain, Norway, and Sweden.

Size: Between 31 & 762mm long
Distribution: Worldwide
Time range: Silurian to Devonian

What About Dinosaurs?

Dinosaurs ruled the Earth for over 160 million years. They came in many shapes and sizes. Most of what we know about the dinosaurs comes from studying fossils of their bones.

Two different groups

Dinosaurs are divided into two major groups according to the way their hip bones were arranged. **Saurischians** (say: *saw-RISH-ee-ans*) were the 'lizard-hipped' dinosaurs. Their lower hip bones fan out where the legs join the hip, like those of lizards. The **Ornithischians** (say: *OAR-nee-THISH-ee-ans*) were the 'bird-hipped' dinosaurs. Their lower hip bones sweep backward.

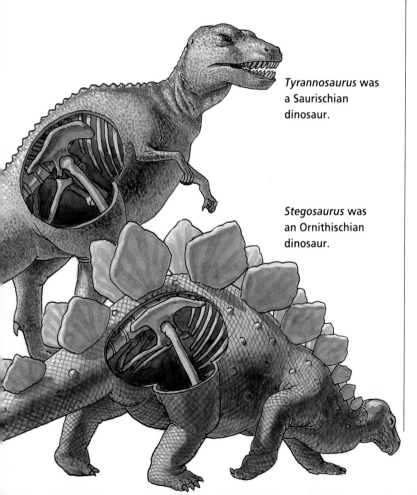

Tyrannosaurus was a Saurischian dinosaur.

Stegosaurus was an Ornithischian dinosaur.

Dinosaur fossils

Tyrannosaurus rex skull

Dinosaur fossils have excited scientists for over a hundred years. Many complete dinosaur skeletons have been found. For others we have only the odd bone or two. The shape and arrangement of the bones can tell us a lot about how dinosaurs lived. Nearly half the known skeletons have been unearthed since the 1940s, so our knowledge has grown tremendously in recent years. Fossils of nests of dinosaur eggs and of baby dinosaurs tell us about how dinosaur mothers looked after their young . A recent exciting discovery was a *Tyrannosaurus* thigh bone that still contained some bone marrow. Maybe the events in *Jurassic Park* are not as impossible as people have said!

Make models of dinosaurs

These simple models will show you how the two kinds of dinosaurs stood and how their weight was balanced. **You will need**: Play-doh, pencils, a clothes-peg, matchsticks, and scissors.

Many of the 'lizard-hipped', Saurischian dinosaurs were two-legged meat-eaters, like *Tyrannosaurus*. The body was quite short and supported by two strong legs. The head had strong jaws packed with razor-sharp teeth, while the long tail balanced the weight of the head. The feet were large for support, but shaped for running.

1 **Mould the Play-doh** into the shape of the *Tyrannosaurus*'s body.
2 **Use a clothes-peg** to represent the heavy jaw.
3 **Use pencils** for the two strong back legs.
4 **Use matchsticks** for the small front limbs.
5 **The long pencil tail balances** the weight of the head at the hips.

Make a dinosaur wall chart

You can make a fascinating dinosaur wall chart decorated with postcards or pictures from magazines and newspapers. Stick them on to a large sheet of card. You might like to divide the chart into 'bird-hipped' and 'lizard-hipped' dinosaurs, or into meat-eaters and plant-eaters.

You could also make a prehistoric time chart. Use a piece of card which is wider than it is high. Divide it into the different geological periods (see the first and last pages of this book). Then paste or glue your pictures of fossils and dinosaurs on to the period in which they lived.

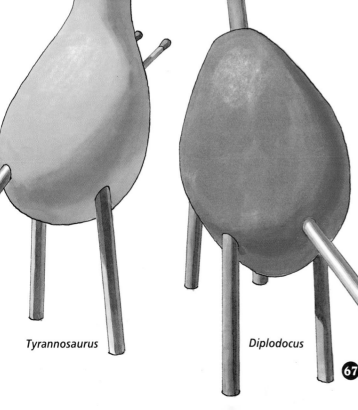

Tyrannosaurus

Diplodocus

The massive plant-eaters

Some of the 'bird-hipped', Ornithischian dinosaurs became plant-eaters. Plant food is difficult to break down and a longer gut is needed, so they had long bodies. They walked on four feet and had long necks for reaching food in high places. They are called 'sauropods'. *Diplodocus* and *Stegosarus* are good examples of this type of dinosaur. Their feet have short bones, splaying out for carrying weight.

1 **Mould the Play-doh** into the shape of the *Diplodocus*'s body.
2 **Use four pencils as legs**. See how they have to be placed differently from those of the *Tyrannosaurus* to make the model stand up.
3 **Use a long pencil for the neck**, and another for the tail.
4 **Make a small head** with a lump of Play-doh.

Vertebrates

Vertebrate is a name that describes all animals with internal backbones. These include fish, amphibians, reptiles, birds, mammals, and human beings.

The first vertebrates were fish which lived during the Silurian Period 440–395 million years ago (mya). They had no jaws, and looked like lampreys, an eel-like modern fish. Fish with jaws developed during the Devonian Period (395–345 mya).

About 350 mya, the first amphibians developed when lung fish (which still exist today) learnt how to survive out of water. Fins developed into stumpy legs and they learned to breathe air directly. They were the dominant (ruling) group on land in the Carboniferous Period (354–280 mya), when the lush swamps and dense vegetation suited them.

Amphibians lay their eggs in water and their young develop there. However, reptiles lay their eggs on land and hatch as miniature adults. The first reptiles appeared during the Carboniferous Period. They resembled lizards, had sharp teeth, and ate insects. From 225 to 65 mya dinosaurs ruled the land – other reptiles dominated the seas.

Fish, amphibians, and reptiles are cold-blooded, while birds and mammals are warm-blooded. Some reptiles, who became extinct about 190 mya, were probably also warm-blooded. Warm-blooded animals do not need the sun's heat for their energy. They are active early in the morning and at night, when cold-blooded animals are not. This is a great advantage when looking for food.

Mammals first appeared in the Triassic Period (225–195 mya), but were small and few in number. It is only at the start of the Tertiary Period (about 65 mya), after the dinosaurs and many invertebrates died out in some kind of catastrophe, that birds and mammals became the dominant groups.

Fish

The most commonly found fossils of creatures with backbones are those of fish. This is because they live in water. Water carries large amounts of sediments and the bodies of dead animals are quickly covered up and preserved. Many fish have bony skeletons and their bodies are protected by tough scales. These parts of their bodies form fossils easily.

Cephalaspis

This fish has a large head-shield which curves backward into two points. There are small eye-holes in the middle of the upper surface and a small mouth underneath. It probably used this for sifting food from the lake or river sediment. Water flowed into the mouth and out through slits behind it. The fish took oxygen from this water with its gills. The body is long and eel-like.

Size: Up to 101mm long
Distribution: Worldwide
Time range: Upper Silurian to Middle Devonian

Gyroptychius

This is an almost complete specimen. The body is covered with small, diamond-shaped scales, but the head is armoured with larger plates. The fish also has two sets of paired fins toward the back of the body and a stumpy tail. It is thought that it swam with an eel-like wriggling movement in fresh water.

Size: This specimen is 70mm long
Distribution: Worldwide
Time range: Devonian

Gosiutichthys

These fish have been preserved in a slab of fine-grained sediment. They were killed when the lake in which they were living dried up. They belong to a modern group of fish known as the 'teleosts'. These fish have bony skeletons and jaws, rayed fins, and swim bladders. Today, there are over 24,000 species in this group. The body of *Gosiutichthys* narrows to a tail which has two lobes of the same size.

Size: Up to 508mm long
Distribution: North America
Time range: Tertiary

Fish

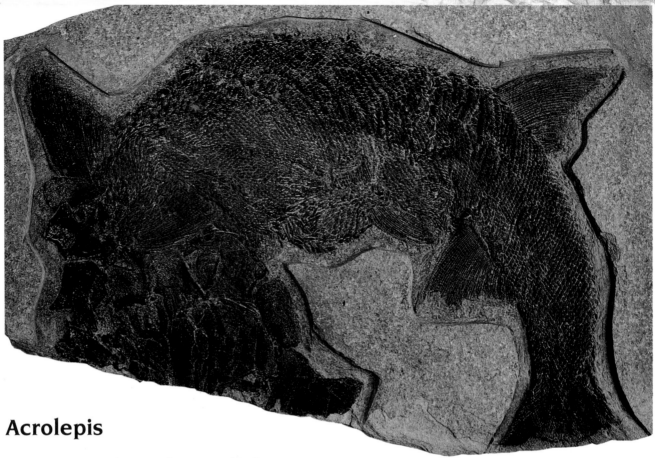

Acrolepis

This specimen has been well preserved in fine-grained sediment, although part of the head and tail are missing. It is a large fish with coarse, diamond-shaped scales. The head is about one fourth of the total length.

Size: Up to 406mm long
Distribution: Britain, Germany, Greenland, & CIS (formerly the USSR)
Time range: Carboniferous to Permian

Platysomus

This specimen is very well preserved in fine-grained limestone. It had cone-shaped teeth, and a deep body covered with scales, which are longer from top to bottom than they are wide. The tail has lobes which are the same length. The fins are triangular and not in pairs. *Platysomus* breathed with gills, and was probably an agile swimmer.

Size: This specimen is 70mm long
Distribution: Europe
Time range: Lower Carboniferous to Upper Permian

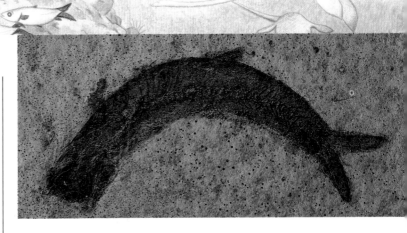

Bothriolepis

The photograph shows the body and head of this fish. Two long, curved spines extend from the head, which is armoured with large plates. These protected the fish from predators that would want to kill and eat it. The rest of the body is eel-like and has no scales. *Bothriolepis* lived on the bottom mud of freshwater lakes.

Size: This specimen is 89mm long
Distribution: Worldwide – Time range: Devonian

Leptolepis

This is another member of the teleost group. *Leptolepis* is a small fish with a long body which narrows toward the tail. The tail has two lobes which are the same size. The small mouth is equipped with many teeth.

Size: Up to 120mm long
Distribution: North America, Europe, Asia, & South Africa
Time range: Upper Triassic to Cretaceous

Dapedius

These fish belong to a group known as the 'holosteans', which are covered with bony plates rather than scales. *Dapedius* has large oblong plates. It has a rounded outline with a long, dorsal fin on its back. The short tail is fan-shaped and there is a long fin below it. The mouth is small and filled with thin, sharp teeth.

Size: Up to 203mm long
Distribution: Europe
Time range: Lower Jurassic

Fossil Teeth

Ptychodus

This is the flat tooth of a shark. It is squarish with a series of ridges running across it. It was probably used to crush bivalves, ammonites, and gastropods. *Ptychodus* comes from a successful group of sharks, which existed for tens of millions of years.

Size: This specimen is 44mm wide
Distribution: North America, Europe, Africa, & Asia
Time range: Cretaceous

Odontaspis

These are the teeth of an ancient shark. It has relatives alive today which reach a length of over 13 feet. The teeth have side cusps, seen as small, sharp points near the base of the tooth, and are made of tough material. They are easily preserved, though they are often found broken.

Size: Average shown 19mm long
Distribution: North & South America, Europe, Asia, Africa, & New Zealand
Time range: Cretaceous to Quaternary

Merycoidodon

This fossil is of some teeth and part of the jaw of a plant-eating mammal sometimes called *Oreodon*. It was a small, pig-like creature with wide molar teeth, like those of cattle, and large upper canine teeth. Four species of this genus have been identified, the main difference between them being their size.

Size: This specimen is 70mm long
Distribution: North America – Time range: Tertiary

Ceratodus

These are the teeth of a lung fish. The teeth are fused into flattened plates, which helped the fish to crush the shelled creatures on which it lived. The surface of the teeth are covered with many small dimples. Present-day lung fish use gills to breathe when under water, but out of the water they use a lung-like bag. They have strong fins for crawling through mud, and can hide in deep burrows during very dry periods.

Size: This specimen is 19mm long
Distribution: Worldwide
Time range: Triassic to Cretaceous

Hyaenanodon

This is part of the lower jaw of a cave hyaena. Such fossils are quite common in sediments not laid down at sea. The teeth are shaped for cutting flesh and crushing bones. The present-day Striped and Brown Hyaenas live in burrows and caves, and feed on animals that have already died. *Hyaenanodon* may have lived in the same way.

Size: This specimen is 82mm long
Distribution: Europe, Asia, and Africa
Time range: Tertiary to Quaternary

Charcarodon

These teeth are the only part of this very large shark which are preserved. They are triangular with two long roots at the base. The edges are jagged for cutting flesh. A present-day relative of this shark is the Great White Shark, which grows to 9m in length. A shark just 6m long weighs 3 tons and has a biting pressure of 20 tons per square inch. *Charcarodon* was probably bigger than a Great White Shark – an adult may have been 15.2m long.

Size: Up to 152mm long
Distribution: Worldwide
Time range: Tertiary

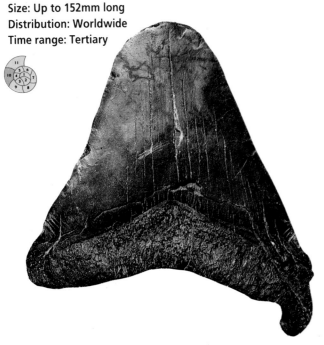

Mammuthus

The photograph shows the cheek tooth of this large elephant-like mammal. The surface is covered with many rough ridges and furrows. This tells us that it was probably a plant-eater. *Mammuthus* was adapted to living in cold conditions – it had a thick coat, a store of food in the form of a hump of fat, small ears, and a large body. These animals were hunted by early humans and are found in prehistoric cave paintings.

Size: This specimen is 254mm long
Distribution: North America, Europe, Asia, and Africa
Time range: Tertiary to Quaternary

Reptiles & Amphibians

Fossils of large reptiles or amphibians are not very common. In some parts of the world, however, many have been found in small areas. It is possible to find single teeth and bones – this is especially true of the large, sea-living reptiles. Many large dinosaur skeletons have been found by amateur fossil collectors.

Iguanodon

This dinosaur walked upright on two strong legs. It is thought that it lived in herds, wandering around the prehistoric landscape eating plants. It has a horny, beak-like mouth and grinding teeth on both sides of the jaw. *Iguanodon* teeth were first found in England in 1815 by an amateur geologist named Dr Gideon Mantell. The specimen on the left in the photograph is part of the dinosaur's backbone; on the right is a toe bone.

Size: Adults grew to about 12.1m tall
Distribution: Europe & north Africa
Time range: Cretaceous

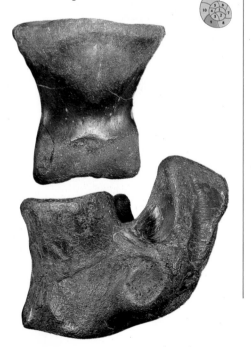

Plesiosaurus

This was a sea-living reptile with a body that was larger and rounder than *Ichthyosaurus*. It was a powerful swimmer, moving through the water by flapping up and down its wide, paddle-like flippers. Some species had very long necks and small heads equipped with sharp teeth. They may have darted their heads at moving prey. Other species had shorter necks and may have been fierce hunters like present-day killer whales.

Size: Top: part of the backbone, 120 mm across; Bottom: rib cage and backbone, section shown about 1.3 m long
Distribution: Worldwide
Time range: Lower Jurassic

Ichthyosaurus

This was a streamlined sea-living reptile. The specimen shown here is a small part of the jaw with teeth. These tell us that this reptile was a meat-eater. Whole skeletons have been found which include an outline of the body. These show that it was similar to present-day dolphins. Adult skeletons have been found which have the skeletons of young inside them. It seems that, like dolphins, *Ichthyosaurus* gave birth to live young.

Size: Adults grew to about 3m long
Distribution: Worldwide
Time range: Triassic to Cretaceous

Temnospondyl

This is the earliest known, complete, amphibian skeleton and was found in West Lothian, Scotland, Great Britain. *Temnospondyl* is not the name of the genus, but of a group of tetrapods (four-limbed vertebrates) into which this specimen has been classified. If you look carefully, you can see that the hind legs have five toes and the front legs have four. It was found in limestone rocks. Other fossils found with it included spiders, scorpions, many-legged creatures and other amphibians, which show that it was living on land, not in water.

Size: This specimen is 406mm long
Distribution: Britain, North America, & Australia
Time range: Lower Carboniferous

Find Out Some More

Useful organizations

The best organization for you to get in touch with, if you want to hunt fossils, is:

RockWATCH, which is a recently-formed subsection of **WATCH**. This is the junior branch of **The Wildlife Trusts**. It is sponsored by the Geologists Association (see below for details about this organization). Local WATCH groups run meetings all over the country.

You can find out about your nearest RockWATCH group by contacting The Wildlife Trusts at The Green, Witham Park, Waterside South, Lincoln LN5 7JR (0522–544400).

The Geologists Association, Burlington House, Piccadilly, London W1V 0JU. They will be able to give amateurs information, and could suggest what to do and where to go.

Your local **natural history society** or **geological society** may organize fossil study days. There may also be a local natural history group you could contact. Your local library will have a list of such societies.

The Dinosaur Society, 84 Moffat Road, Waban, Massachusetts 02168, USA. This society works to promote accurate scientific information about dinosaurs and to promote the work of artists who paint scientifically accurate pictures of the dinosaurs. They co-operate in the publication of *Dino Times* a monthly newspaper for children.

Field Studies Council, Central Services, Preston Montford, Montford Bridge, Shrewsbury, Shropshire SY4 1HW (0743–850674). They run interesting courses for families at ten Field Centres throughout England and Wales. They also run many courses for school groups; ask your teacher about these.

In Scotland, contact the **Scottish Field Studies Association**, Kindrogan Field Centre, Enochdhu, Blairgowrie, Perthshire PH10 7PG (0250–881286).

National Trust for Places of Historic Interest or Natural Beauty, 36 Queen Anne's Gate, London SW1H 9AS (071–222 9251). They own more than 570 properties and over 232,000 hectares of unspoiled countryside throughout England, Wales and Northern Ireland, including over 850 kilometres of coastline. They run many courses for school groups; ask your teacher to find out about these.

In Scotland, contact **The National Trust for Scotland** (care of the Education Adviser), 5 Charlotte Square, Edinburgh EH2 4DU (031–226 5922).

Useful books

Cambridge Field Guide to Prehistoric Life by David Lambert (Cambridge University Press, 1989).

Dictionary of Geology, D.G.A. Whitten with J.R.V. Brooks (Penguin, 1972). Useful reference book explaining many technical terms.

Dinosaur! by Dr David Norman (Boxtree, 1991.) The author is the Director of the Sedgwick Museum.

Dinosaurs, A Global View by S.J. Czerkas & S.A. Czerkas (Dragon's World, 1990).

The Pocket Guide to Fossils by Chris Pellant (Dragon's World, 1992). A useful spiral-bound guide for collectors.

Hamlyn Guide to Minerals, Rocks & Fossils by R. Hamilton (Hamlyn, 1992).

Fossils, Rock & Mineral (Dorling Kindersley, 1991). One of the Eyewitness guides.

Fossils in Colour by J.F. Kirkaldy (Blandford Press, 1980). An illustrated identification guide to all groups of fossils.

Geologists Association Guides Nos 1–41 (Geologists Association, see previous column)

The Pocket Guide to Rocks and Minerals, Michael O'Donoghue (Dragon's World, 1990). Spiral-bound guide showing over 260 specimens.

Index & Glossary

Places to visit:

British Museum of Natural History, Cromwell Road, London SW7. This museum has the most comprehensive dinosaur exhibition in Britain, and a huge collection of fossil plants and animals.

National Museum of Wales, Cathays Park, Cardiff, CF1 3NP. This museum has a collection of Welsh fossil plants and animals, minerals and rocks.

Royal Museum of Scotland, Chambers Street, Edinburgh EH1 1JF. This museum has important collections of fossils and minerals.

Sedgwick Museum of Geology, Cambridge. This museum has fossil fragments of around a dozen dinosaurs, as well as plaster reconstructions of some dinosaurs.

Museum of Isle of Wight Geology, Isle of Wight.

Oxford University Museum, Parks Road, Oxford. This museum has a good collection of fossil bones and a plaster cast of a dinosaur skeleton.

Index & Glossary

Endorsed by WATCH:

WATCH is the national wildlife and environmental club for young people. It is the junior section of The Wildlife Trusts, the largest voluntary organization in the United Kingdom, which is dedicated to protecting our wildlife and wild places.

   WATCH groups throughout the United Kingdom take part in exciting national projects and play an active role in nature conservation. WATCH members receive the club magazine WATCHWORD three times a year. It is packed full with ideas, projects and articles explaining current environmental concerns.

   For further information, please send a stamped addressed envelope to the address below.

The Green
Witham Park
Waterside South
Lincoln
LN5 7JR

The Geological Periods of the Earth

Pre-Cambrian

1 Cambrian
600–500 million years ago

2 Ordovician
500–440 million years ago

3 Silurian
440–395 million years ago

4 Devonian
395–345 million years ago

5 Carboniferous
345–280 million years ago

6 Permian
280–225 million years ago

Paleozoic Era

7 Triassic
225–190 million years ago

8 Jurassic
190–136 million years ago